SIMPLE
CONFUCIANISM

A Guide to Living Virtuously

SIMPLE
CONFUCIANISM

A Guide to Living Virtuously

C. Alexander Simpkins Ph.D. • Annellen Simpkins Ph.D.

Tuttle Publishing
Boston • Rutland, Vermont • Tokyo

First published in 2000 by Tuttle Publishing, an imprint of Periplus Editions (HK) Ltd, with editorial offices at 153 Milk Street, Boston, Massachusetts 02109.

LIBRARY OF CONGRESS CATALOGING-IN-PUBLICATION DATA
WILL BE FOUND AT THE END OF THIS BOOK.

Distributed by

USA
Tuttle Publishing
Distribution Center
Airport Industrial Park
364 Innovation Drive
North Clarendon, VT 05759-9436
Tel: (802) 773-8930
Tel: (800) 526-2778

JAPAN
Tuttle Publishing
RK Building, 2nd Floor
2-13-10 Shimo-Meguro, Meguro-Ku
Tokyo 153 0064
Tel: (03) 5437-0171
Fax: (03) 5437-0755

CANADA
Raincoast Books
8680 Cambie Street
Vancouver, British Columbia
V6P 6M9
Tel: (604) 323-7100
Fax: (604) 323-2600

SOUTHEAST ASIA
Berkeley Books Pte Ltd
5 Little Road #08-01
Singapore 536983
Tel: (65) 280-1330
Fax: (65) 280-6290

First edition
06 05 04 03 02 01 00   10 9 8 7 6 5 4 3 2 1

Printed in the Uunited States of America

We dedicate this book to our parents and ancestors, and to
all parents and ancestors whose wisdom reaches out from the
past to guide us today.

Carmen Z. Simpkins' abstract expressionist paintings suggest
mood, movement, and mysticism. Simpkins has been painting
for seventy-five years. Her first solo show took place in
Camden, Maine, in 1962 at the Broadlawn Gallery. She has
exhibited throughout the world, and her works are in private
collections in Europe and America. Her work is on display
at her gallery in Clinton, South Carolina.

CONTENTS

INTRODUCTION

Confucian philosophy has had a profound effect on Asian society and politics for many centuries, but its effects have also been felt by the entire world. Ralph Waldo Emerson lauded Confucius as "the George Washington of the world of thought" (Chang 1957, 112). Voltaire said that "to realize the theories of Confucius would bring about the happiest and most valuable period of human history" (Chang 1957, 110). Confucianism addresses how people should live with each other at their best, regardless of their life-situation, and points to an inner source of guidelines to follow for conduct.

A recent poll conducted by the Pew Research Center asked one thousand five hundred Americans how they felt about life-changes over the past one hundred years. The results showed that many Americans are feeling a deficit in their lives. "They describe it in various ways: an absence of morality, a loss of innocence, a lack of trust in others." As one person said, "Life may have gotten better, but people haven't" (Lester 1999). Confucianism is a penetrating philosophy that delves deeply into these issues, offering a Path to reclaim lost values. Anyone can develop their humanity and become a sage. Virtue breeds nobility. It is a matter of character. People can become the best they can be through fully and sincerely engaging in living their lives according to true values.

Confucianism is a way to live an ethical and intelligent life even though the world around us is in turmoil. We can learn how to get along better with ourselves, our families, our work, and in the greater society while carrying out our individual destiny within the larger pattern of the universe. Most important, we can find happiness and fulfillment by developing ourselves in the fullest sense of our humanity, in tune with the Confucian Way.

ABOUT THIS BOOK

Simple Confucianism opens the doorway to using the ancient wisdom of Confucius and his followers in your everyday life. The book is divided into three parts. Part One gives the background and development of the philosophy, highlighting pivotal people. Part Two explains key themes expressed as concepts, virtues, and lifestyles. Part Three shows ways to bring the wisdom, happiness, and harmony of this philosophy into your own life.

PART I

Confucianism In Time

If Here and Now
Are all that matter
Then life means
Little but scattered
Fragments.
From ideas,
And memories
Of time's lost ways,
Search for more meaning
Than just today's.
—C. Alexander Simpkins

When we learn of Confucius, we share in his spirit and the work of his followers who help develop and perpetuate this dynamic philosophy. Thanks to the many scholars who have devoted their thoughts to Confucianism, these ideas have had an enduring influence that is felt around the world. Legends interweave with facts as the early beginnings unfold.

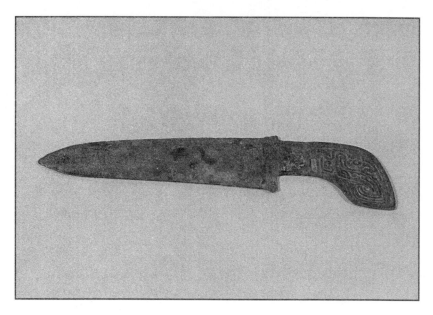

Ko (with stylized bird on handle), 14th–11th century B.C., Late Shang period, Bronze. San Diego Museum of Art (Gift of C.T. Loo, Inc.) *The Ko was a standard Shang weapon.*

CHAPTER 1

Origins

*In the ways prescribed by the ancient kings, this is the excellent
quality, and in things small and great we follow them.*
—Confucius, *Analects* 1-12

BACKGROUND OF CONFUCIUS'S WORLD

Historical research confirms that China's earliest dynasty, the Shang
(1751–1112 B.C.), began during the Bronze Age. Chinese society at this time
consisted of widely scattered tribes who believed the people's lives were ruled
by spiritual beings and mystical forces.

The Shang gave way to the Chou dynasty (1111–249 B.C.) and feudal-
ism, which unified the country into a hierarchical social structure. The Chou
was the longest-lived dynasty in Chinese history. These rulers were no longer
considered gods. For them, power came with virtue(*te*), not from mystical
forces or spiritual beings. They drew their authority from the Mandate of
Heaven, an ancient doctrine based on the idea that the cosmos was domi-
nated by an impersonal yet all-powerful heaven. Rulers were responsible for

guiding people using a moral code which stated that it was how people lived and what people did that determined their fate. Humanity developed with progress in the trades, the arts, and education. Humanism had found a home in Chinese culture, and Confucius would eventually become one of its greatest spokesmen.

Beginning in the fifth century B.C., civil wars and intense rivalries among the many small kingdoms finally brought about the end of the Chou dynasty. And it was during these unsettled times that Confucius lived. Later, Confucius would look back fondly on the earlier years of the Chou dynasty as a period of nobility and morality.

LEGENDARY ORIGINS

Confucius drew his ideas from both actual history and the shadowy mythical history that predated the Shang. Although there is no archaeological evidence for it, legends are very detailed and widely accepted. Much like the American legends of Johnny Appleseed and Daniel Webster, people whose many incredible achievements were admired, it is not known whether the ancient Chinese culture-heroes actually existed. Still, the stories surrounding them inspire hope and encourage people to fulfill their better natures. Confucians referred to these ancient kings not only as enlightened leaders but also as outstanding human beings.

The oldest of these wise kings were known as the Three Sovereigns: Fu-hsi, the Ox-tamer (2852 B.C.); Shen-nung, the Divine Farmer (2737 B.C.); and Huang-ti, the Yellow Emperor (2607 B.C.). Huang-ti is not only revered by the Confucians but also held in high esteem by the Taoists. His reign is given credit for introducing writing, wooden houses, silk, boats, and carts. He was also thought to have invented healing methods that were later incorporated into Eastern medicine.

Huang-ti was the first in a series of emperors who brought civilization to even higher development. Yao (who reigned from 2356 to 2347 B.C.); Shun

(2244–2205 B.C.); and Yü, who began ruling in 2205 B.C. were known as the Three Sage Kings. Confucius idealized these leaders and their accomplishments, often holding them up as examples for government and culture to follow. According to Confucius, Yao introduced the use of rituals and music to help cultivate the person. When it came time for Yao to choose a successor, he passed over his unworthy son and chose, instead, a poor peasant named Shun because he was virtuous. Thus, Yao exemplified the Confucian value of giving a reward based on merit.

Shun's rule was plagued by floods until he found a man named Yü, who devoted ten years of single-minded effort searching for a way to turn the tides of the overflowing waters. Yü devised and implemented a successful, nationwide system—becoming one of the world's first official engineers! Shun was so moved by Yü's loyal, wholehearted devotion to saving the country that he appointed Yü his successor. Once again, virtuous action was recognized and given the highest position in government.

The dynasty that began with Yü's rule was called the Hsia. For centuries, from 2205-1751 B.C., the Hsia rulers continued to develop a cultured social order. Then, in 1751 B.C , they were overthrown by Chich, the founder of the Shang dynasty.

ANCIENT TEXTS

The oldest written works in Chinese history are contained in the *Book of History* and the *Book of Odes*. Historians believe that the *Book of History*, which did not survive the Ch'in dynasty's (221-207 B.C.) devastating book burnings, may not be the original work (see page 30). The *Book of Odes*, however, being a collection of songs, is considered more authentically ancient, since music was passed along from memory, sung aloud by one generation to the next. Both of these books became part of the thirteen Confucian classics (see Chapter 4).

The *Book of History* was said to be a collection of documents from the legendary emperors Yao, Shun, and Yü and is the first book that Confucius edited. It contains wise sayings of advice and lofty regulations from the sage kings and their ministers. The spirit of the work is ethical, including how to govern by virtue. For example, "Let the King be serious in what he does. He should not neglect to be serious with virtue" (Chan 1963, 38). Although the book may not be as old as Confucius claimed, it did inspire some of his concepts.

The *Book of Odes, Shih Ching*, is the most reliable and best preserved work of Chinese literature. Historians recognize this as an authentic text. It is a collection of approximately three hundred poems and songs from the early Chou dynasty and some even from the earlier Shang period. Confucius gathered the best out of thousands, thereby preserving this poetic and musical tradition that might have otherwise been lost. He interpreted the lyrics and discussed them daily with his students, using the songs and poems to transmit Confucian teachings. This poem shows clearly the essence of Confucian philosophy:

> *I am (but as) a little child,*
> *Without intelligence to be reverently (attentive to my duties);*
> *I will learn to hold fast the gleams (of knowledge), till I arrive at bright*
> *   intelligence.*
> *Assist me to bear the burden (of my position),*
> *And show me how to display a virtuous conduct.*

(Wilhelm 1931, 121)

CHAPTER 2

Confucius: The First Teacher

Confucius said, I cannot claim to have discovered wisdom and virtue.
What I can say is that I never waver on the path I pursue and am tireless
in my efforts to teach others—this and nothing more.
—Paraphrased from Confucius, *Analects*

Confucius stands out as one of the supremely great figures in the history of the world. Even European philosopher Karl Jaspers grouped him in his book of great philosophers with Socrates, Buddha, and Jesus. Yet Confucius would have been the first to say that he was just a man like any other. Still, his ideas inspire us to express our better natures, and it is perhaps this effect that makes him so important to humanity.

Confucius was born in the state of Lu, in the district of Ch'ang P'ing, in the city of Chou. His ancestors were from the state of Sung. Confucius's father, K'ung Shû-Lîang Hêh, was a warrior-soldier, and some sources say a governor of Chou. Chinese historian Ssu-ma Ch'ien (145–86 B.C.) gives an account of the birth of Confucius in *The Grand Scribe's Record*. Confucius's

**Confucius Statue. Utmost sage; Foremost teacher.
Bronze, 7'4" tall. San Diego Chinese Historical Museum.
Presented by former Minister of Education Kao Wei-Fang.**

father was already an older man and married to a woman who had given him nine daughters. Anxious for a son to continue the family line, he asked for the hand of a younger woman, Chang-tsâi, in marriage. After the wedding, she went with her new husband to a hill called Ni-chiû, where they prayed in a grove for a son. Chang-tsâi then went up the hill alone. All the leaves on the trees stood up, then bowed down as she returned. That night in her dreams the Dark Lord of Ti came to her and told her that she would have a son who would be a sage. He instructed her to give birth in a hollow mulberry tree.

When Chang-tsâi was ready to deliver her baby, she could not find the right tree, but instead located a cave known as the Hollow Mulberry Tree. There she gave birth to her son, Confucius. A bubbling spring magically appeared in the cave on the twenty-first day of the tenth month of the twentieth year of Emperor Ling in the year 551 B.C. After Confucius was bathed, the spring sank back into the ground and disappeared. Confucius was born with a large bump on his forehead, which may have led to his being named Ch'iu (hill). His family name was K'ung. So his full name was K'ung Ch'iu. Traditionally, he came to be known as Grand Master K'ung, or K'ung Fu-tzu (*tzu* means master), which has been latinized to Confucius. Confucius's father died when his son was only three years old.

Because his father had been a retainer of the Mengs, Confucius was taken under the wing of the Meng family, one of the three main families of Lu. Confucius did not formally attend school, but according to tradition, this was not unusual. Before Confucius there were no public schools, only private tutors training the children of aristocrats for statecraft and instructing archivists and historians about cultural and social ceremonies.

Confucius was married at nineteen and had a son when he was twenty. He named his son Li Po-yu, which means carp, because the duke of Chou had given him a carp as a gift. Ever after, the carp has been an emblem of Confucianism. Po-yu died at fifty, so Confucius, who lived to age seventy-five, outlived him. Po-yu's son, Tzse-sze, became one of Confucius's best students.

Even though Confucius lost his son early, his grandson carried the philosophy forward. Tzse-sze was the author of *The Doctrine of the Mean*, one of the primary Confucian classics.

As a young man with little money, Confucius took on a few minor offices in the civil service and excelled at them. But except for taking occasional positions such as minister of finance and minister of justice in his middle years, Confucius chose to keep his time mostly free for instructing.

Confucius began to teach when he was twenty-two and had students immediately, opening the doors of his school to anyone who was sincerely willing to learn. His fees were low, charging only what the student could afford. One student paid him with a bundle of dried meat! Confucius transferred his love of learning and ideals to his students and taught them how to think for themselves. As he said: "When I have presented one corner of a subject to anyone and he cannot from it learn the other three, I do not repeat my lesson" (*Analects* 7–7, in Legge 1971, 61).

Confucius devoted his life to teaching. Over his lifetime he taught some three thousand students. The names of seventy-two of his best are still remembered today. They were instrumental in recording his sayings and carrying his work forward. It is apparent why Confucius is regarded as the First Teacher in China. Music became an important interest for Confucius, and he began to study it in depth at the age of twenty-nine. While he played and listened to music he experienced a profound alteration in his thoughts and feelings. Eventually Confucius integrated music into his philosophy, showing its ability to influence people for better or worse.

Confucius consulted Lao-tzu, the legendary founder of Taoism and author of the *Tao Te Ching*, to learn how to conduct ceremonies and music. Lao-tzu was the Royal Librarian scribe and fifty years older than Confucius. The link between Taoism and Confucianism was foreshadowed in their consultations. While the two schools of philosophy quarreled off and on for many years, Taoism and Confucianism eventually evolved new interpretations that incorporated elements of each other, as reflected in the later Neo-Confucian and Neo-Taoist movements. Each had something the other lacked.

Philosophers commonly traveled to neighboring provinces to teach and advise in philosophy. So Confucius decided to instruct the governments of surrounding areas and brought a group of his students with him. He talked to many different princes; some listened and cared, others did not. A number of the entries in the *Analects*—a collection of Confucius's sayings—describe these discussions. After fourteen years of an itinerant lifestyle, at the age of sixty-eight Confucius returned to Lu, where he spent his last years teaching, occasionally advising government, and, of course, always learning. In his last years, he edited the *I Ching*.

Both Taoists and Confucians revered the *I Ching* as primary to understanding the inner workings of the universe. Confucius wrote a commentary on each hexagram. Known as the *Ten Wings*, it served as the basis for the Neo-Confucians, their theory in conceptual metaphor being drawn from the *I Ching*. Confucius also wrote a definitive history of his own era, called the *Spring and Autumn Annals*.

Confucius was a large man with a gentle disposition who enjoyed music and dance. An entry in the *Analects* characterized him as friendly but dignified, grand but not fierce, respectful while also relaxed (paraphrased from *Analects* 7–37). He offered his own autobiography:

> At 15, I had set my mind on learning. At 30, I could stand on my own feet. At 40, I was determined not to be led astray by irrelevancies. At 50, I fully realized what destiny had in store for me. At 60, I could follow a truth without fuss. At 70, I could let my action follow my heart's desire without transgressing the standards of right. (Chang 1957, 14)

Confucius was a man brought up in humble circumstances who, rather than compromise his integrity, steadfastly held to his ideals and beliefs. During

Confucius was a warm and kindly sage.

the turmoil of China's upheavals, instead of withdrawing to meditate in solitude, Confucius engaged in his world. He tirelessly taught his many faithful followers, disciples who carried on his tradition. He did his best to live consistent with his doctrines, teaching by example, in humility and discipline.

CONFUCIUS'S THOUGHT

Confucius's thought was not systematic by Western standards, but that was not his goal. He was attempting to set a standard for all subsequent Confucian philosophers in China. He believed in searching inwardly, not in setting out a system to imitate. He had faith that his followers would develop the wisdom for future generations. Truth's implications are not bound by time.

Confucius addressed the problem of the human condition. He emphasized the intimate links between the Way of Heaven and the Way of Earth with the Way of Humanity. He put the world of action in social relationships at the center. Confucians point to everyday life as the focus of meditation to find enlightenment. Confucius said,

> *I used to devote myself to thinking, doing without food throughout the day and without sleep throughout the night. I found that the practice was without merit; the better way is to learn. (Chang 1957, 13)*

CONFUCIAN VIRTUES

Nobility is a function of how we live. What we are in character is molded by what we do. Our actions matter and can lead to social harmony, expressed in tradition, honor, and virtue. Confucius distinguished a number of virtues: humanness (*jen*), filial piety, loyalty, duty, sincerity, righteousness, and propriety.

The most central virtue is human-heartedness, jen. This primary quality was interpreted in various ways by the generations that followed Confucius. Jen translates as true personhood, being fully human. The true self is honest, forthright, correct. These qualities are the givens of humanity. All we need to do is to be true, genuine, and sincere, and Confucius taught his students to cultivate these qualities.

Virtues are action-oriented, practiced in relationship with others and in relationship to oneself, even when you are alone. To Confucius, human beings use values to guide their lives. Therefore, the wise person does not attempt to separate reality from value. "Is" includes "ought." We act toward others and our actions affect them in positive or negative ways. In the process, our actions assume value to us and others.

To the question often posed in Zen—Is enlightenment sudden or the product of gradual cultivation?—Confucius would answer: continual gradual cultivation. Everyone has the potential for being and living enlightened. But sages continually cultivate the way in everyday life and relationships, lest the light be smothered and dimmed. Immorality and insincerity are not innate. They are learned. So social influences and life's circumstances can guide us down the wrong path. Confucius taught that we can and should always return to our original, good, human nature.

This world as we live it—with our duties, family, responsibilities, and obligations—is the appropriate focus. *Shu* (reciprocity) expresses the Confucian version of the golden rule, sometimes called the silver rule, to not do to others what you would not have done to you. Ideals are to be found in this world, in everyday life and relationships. By not doing what is imperfect and incorrect, correctness can be found, perfection comes. Jen is a quality to be cultivated in oneself and sought in others.

The Confucian emphasis on virtue raises the question of whether virtuous living is really possible. Confucius believed that reflections of jen could be found in the classical traditions when virtue was embodied by the early sage kings. He believed that virtue can be found, taught, and developed amid the realities of life. But the source is always discovered for each person within.

The great learning takes root in clarifying the way wherein the intelligence increases through the process of looking straight into one's own heart and acting on the results. (Pound 1951, 27)

By his unselfish devotion to his ideals, Confucius's teaching transcended his life and became an inseparable part of China's great civilization and culture for all time. Twenty-five hundred years after his life, his spirit still speaks to us through his dialogues and commentaries, as well as through the insights of his students. The wisdom of Confucius is timeless and has affected the world throughout history. The Neo-Confucians returned to the cultural treasure of his ideas for inspiration, and most Chinese philosophies have since incorporated some aspect of his thought into theirs. Just as all Western psychology had to come to terms with Freud, Eastern philosophy in turn had to come to terms with Confucius. Confucius set the standard against which we measure ourselves, to compare and contrast, and in so doing, to learn.

CHAPTER 3

Mencius: Cherishing the Goodness Within

Mencius said, When we do not, by what we do, realize what we desire, we must turn inwards, and examine ourselves in every point.
—*Book of Mencius,* in James Legge,
The Works of Mencius

Mencius (371–289 B.C.) is considered by most historians to be the second great Confucian. He carried Confucianism forward, adding his own unique contributions.

A contemporary of Aristotle, Mencius lived during a period of political chaos in China, similar to the day of Confucius. Many small kingdoms fought back and forth for power and land, causing great unrest and hardships for the ordinary citizen. Six philosophical schools (Confucians, Yin-yang School, Mohists, Logicians, Legalists, and Taoists) offered rationales and solutions for the social problems. Mencius hoped to have a sane influence on this chaotic environment with his positive and optimistic Confucianism.

EARLY YEARS

Mencius was born in the same region as Confucius. His name was really Mang-tsu, but it has since been latinized as the more familiar Mencius. Mencius's father married his mother late in his life and died when Mencius was very young. Mencius's mother, whose maiden name was Chang, was a remarkable woman, described as a model of what a mother should be. When Mencius was young, he lived in a house located near a cemetery. His mother watched him as he played, acting out the funeral rituals he witnessed from his window. Realizing "This is no place for my son," she moved to a house close to the marketplace. Now Mencius pretended that he was a merchant, buying and selling. Once again, his mother said, "This is no place for my son." Finally, she found a home next to the school. Now Mencius pretended to be a scholar. "At last!" his mother said. "*This* is the proper place for my son."

Mencius's mother encouraged her son to be serious about his education. One day when Mencius returned home from school his mother looked up from her weaving and asked, "How was your day?"

Mencius answered indifferently, as adolescents often will, "Well enough."

Responding to his attitude, she took a knife and cut the thread she was working on. Mencius was surprised and asked, "Why did you do that?"

"I neglect my thread just as you neglect your learning!" She proceeded to lecture him on the importance of wholehearted study. The boy took her advice and became a serious student. Mencius eventually married and had a family of his own, but he maintained a close relationship with his mother throughout his life.

PROFESSIONAL LIFE

Mencius studied Confucianism under a disciple of Tzse-sze, Confucius's grandson. He felt that Confucius's teachings permeated his spirit: "Although I could not be a disciple of Confucius myself, I have endeavored to cultivate my character and knowledge by means of others who were" (Legge 1970, 14).

Little is known about Mencius's early years of professional life, although most historians believe he was a teacher. He tried to get the local government to accept his ideas, but found that no one would listen. This prompted Mencius to travel to neighboring states where he did interest many rulers in his ideas. He recorded his conversations with princes and kings, and they are central to his writings.

Mencius advised leaders to sincerely care about their people. He taught that if the ruler was benevolent and fostered other's lives, the people would give their full support to the government. Mencius did not believe that kings should rule by force. Heaven gives the mandate to rulers to rule. If they rule by benevolence and justice, people would naturally remain loyal. If not, rulers violate their mandate, and the people have a right to rebel. He advised the leaders to begin with kindness.

Mencius believed in many democratic principles. He proposed that all people are equal, and that the will and welfare of the people is the essence of the state. What the people say is primary. The ruler should share resources with the people, ruling by the heart, not the sword. Dictatorial government eventually fails.

Eventually Mencius retired from advising governments to live quietly. Some historians believe that this was the period when he wrote about his years of interactions and his views on many topics. These writings ring as true for us today as they did for the people of his day. Mencius lived a long life, dying at age eighty-four. He left a thoughtful legacy to guide us toward positive values, even when times are difficult.

CHANGE BEGINS WITHIN

You cannot change the problems of the world without first changing yourself. Many of the hardships we endure in life are self-inflicted to some extent. As Mencius said, "When heaven sends down calamities it is still possible to escape them. When we occasion the calamities ourselves, it is not possible any longer to live" (Legge 1970, 299).

The conflicts and problems we have in our psyches are reflected and even magnified when others react to us. Mencius explained how this comes about with an example from a children's song.

> *When the water of the Ts'ang-lang is clear*
> *I wash the strings of my cap in it*
> *When the water of the Ts'ang-lang is muddy,*
> *I use it to wash my feet.*
> (Paraphrased from the *Book of Mencius* in Legge 1970, 299)

The quality of the water determines how people use it. When it is clean, people keep it clean; but when the water is dirty, people make it dirtier. Similarly, Mencius believed that if people despise themselves, then others will despise them. We bring about many of our problems by how we think and feel about ourselves. Conversely, if we are to learn to respect others, we must first respect ourselves. Negative feelings about ourselves lower us into the mire of conflicts and confusion. Confucianism guides us to higher ground.

As in most of the Eastern philosophies, Mencius turns us to our own mind as the place to begin. In Zen Buddhism, meditation is the key to enlightenment. Taoists use meditation to bring about inner calm and tranquillity. Any change we wish to make in our lives must begin with what the Confucians call "cultivating the mind." Mencius explained,

> *Anyone who really wishes to grow a small tree like the t'ung or szu tree learns how to tend it. But in the matter of one's own person, there are those who do not learn how to tend it, not so much because they have a greater love for a tree than for themselves, but because of a heedlessness that is very deep-seated. (Mencius in Dobson 1969, 145–46)*

Developing self-awareness is the first step. Mencius recognized that people often function with very little awareness of themselves and of their actions. "Most people do things without knowing what they do, and go on doing them without any thought as to what they are doing. They do this all their lives without ever understanding the Way" (Mencius in Dobson 1969, 147).

HUMAN NATURE IS GOOD

Mencius boldly stated that human nature is good. He believed that all people share a common feeling that they cannot bear to see others suffer. He argued that people, from the most nobly refined to the worst behaved, will feel concern for a child in danger. One of his favorite examples was how everyone would have a feeling of horror and distress on seeing a child about to fall into a well.

Some argued with Mencius, saying that if human nature is so good, why is there so much evil in the world? How could Mencius's theory explain why people act with malice? Mencius answered that though human nature is good at heart, sometimes people turn away from the positive without even realizing it. Life experiences affect them. They lose touch with the Way.

Mencius gave an example of an area that was known for being ugly and barren called Bull Mountain. Long ago, before most people remembered, Bull Mountain was covered with beautiful trees. But as the state expanded, people chopped down the trees for wood, and the mountain lost its beauty. Despite this destruction, nature took its course and fresh plants began to grow, covering the mountain once again with greenery. But then people sent their livestock to graze on the mountain, which stripped it once again of its beauty. "Now just as the natural state of the mountain was quite different from what now appears, so too in every man (little though they may be apparent) there assuredly were once feelings of decency and kindness. . . . What chance then has our nature, any more than that mountain, of keeping its beauty?" (Mencius in Waley 1946, 117).

Mencius was optimistic about human potential, believing that while negative environmental influences may divert us from our innate goodness, we can always bring it back, and that people possess intuitive knowledge about right and wrong. The important and sometimes difficult task is to discover the right path and then to follow it. "Let a man not do what his own sense of righteousness tells him not to do, and let him not desire what his sense of righteousness tells him not to desire—to act thus is all he has to do" (Legge 1970, 457).

We can all cultivate our better nature, according to Mencius. This is one of the very positive aspects of Confucian philosophy. All are capable of change. Anyone can live a happy and fulfilling life, without worry, by following the correct Path. "Therefore the True Gentleman spends a lifetime of careful thought, but not a day in worrying" (Mencius in Dobson 1969, 134).

THE SUPERIOR PERSON

The superior person is the "person of jen." Similar to Confucius, Mencius believed jen to be the attribute of being human at its very best. Jen is what distinguishes us from animals—the ability to behave with benevolence, love, and respect.

The sage is benevolent and respectful. To develop ourselves, we must search for our own inborn benevolence and feelings of respect, rooted in heart. Following the Confucian Way encourages people to get in touch with their nature so they will sincerely and genuinely feel these qualities. Correct action easily follows when the heart is sincere.

Thus persons of jen fill their thoughts with love and respect. Mencius believed that when we love and sincerely respect humanity, goodness is returned to us. "The man of Humanity loves others. . . . He who loves others is in turn loved by others." We should also respect others. "The man of propriety respects others. . . . He who respects others is in turn respected by others" (Mencius in Dobson 1969, 133).

The practice of these qualities begins with your own family, especially your parents. Filial piety was an important value to the Confucians. They felt a duty to love and respect their parents. As Mencius explained, if everyone simply treated their own parents with love and respect, many of the world's problems would disappear. Mencius, like Confucius, did not expect us to treat everyone with the same intensity of love. The farther removed we are from our immediate family, hometown, and country, the less personal and intense are our emotions for them, but the general intent is always benevolent and respectful. The Lu-Wang School of Neo-Confucianism would extend filial piety more generously, as the basic model for all relationships.

THE CLASSICAL STANDARD TO GUIDE US

Accomplishing this may seem like trying to steer a boat, lost in the middle of a stormy sea, back to shore. How can we guide ourselves back to our better nature if we have lost it? Mencius recognized the difficulties and pointed people to the best in history for a model to follow. We can look back

Li Earthenware: Ceramic Jar (with stand), 12th-11th century B.C. Late Shang period, early Chou dynasty. San Diego Museum of Art (Bequest of Emile Leonard Schoppe) *This three-legged round jar was known as a "li." The li-shaped pottery was so useful that it continued to be produced continuously for 1000 years.*

to great leaders of the past to help guide our actions today. Like Confucius, Mencius drew from the great sage kings—Yao, Shun, and Yü—as well as from some of the rulers of the Chou dynasty.

Most people today look to the future as the source of their hopes and the fulfillment of their dreams. Tomorrow will be better, they think. But the Confucians looked backward to the past. They thought yesterday was better, and that if people reclaim the wisdom from the past, they too can become wise. Classical Confucians find hope for humanity today in knowing that people have been wise and virtuous in the past.

CHAPTER 4

Classic Confucianism Evolves

*Hsün-tzu said, Not always is outward misfortune an evil; it can
be a test. . . . There are cases in which men rise from desperate
circumstances to the highest calling.*
—Karl Jaspers, *Socrates, Buddha, Confucius, Jesus*

HSÜN-TZU

As Confucianism evolved, it diverged into two streams. Mencius carried
forth Confucius's emphasis on our good human nature, filled with potential.
Hsün-tzu (298–238 B.C.), another Confucian, took a different path. He said
that human nature is fundamentally evil but correctable. Even though he
achieved some renown in his own time, Hsün-tzu's work has not been
included as part of the Confucian classics. Perhaps this is due to Hsün-tzu's
lack of faith in human nature.

EARLY YEARS

Hsün-tzu lived at the end of the Warring States Period (480-221 B.C.) that had so disturbed Mencius. His personal name was K'uang and was sometimes referred to as Ch'ing, but he was known as Master Hsün, or Hsün-tzu. Very little is known about him until he was approximately fifty years old, when he journeyed to the state of Chi to take on residency as part of the royal family's scholar program.

King Hsüan (reigned 342–324 B.C.) tried to raise the prestige of Chi by funding scholars to live at his royal court. They offered free room and board as well as honors and titles. Scholars flocked to Chi, making it a great center for learning. Even Mencius had visited Chi during his travels. By the time Hsün-tzu arrived, around 264 B.C., a new generation of scholars were being sought. Hsün-tzu was welcomed and honored. But he eventually antagonized some of the other philosophers and was forced to leave. He traveled next to Chu.

Hsün-tzu was offered a post as magistrate in a small province of Chu called Lang-ling. This position did not last too long because the ruler who had given Hsün-tzu the position was assassinated by rivals in 238 B.C. Hsün-tzu, however, remained in this area, teaching and writing, for the remainder of his life.

EVIL NATURE

Hsün-tzu disagreed with Mencius's belief that human nature is fundamentally good. He believed human nature is bad, but that positive activities could make people become good. He asserted that people are born with certain feelings, impulses, and desires to hate and envy others, and if left unchecked, these innate negative tendencies would lead to disaster. To Hsün-tzu, these tendencies were inevitable. "Nature is what is given by Heaven; you cannot learn it, you cannot acquire it by effort" (Watson 1969, 158). These negative human traits, Hsün-tzu believed, are our Life-situation.

Learning is the hope for humankind. People can become civilized through good teachers and an evolved culture. Unlike Confucius and

Mencius, who thought education led to the refining of our nature, Hsün-tzu believed that education served to steer evil nature toward goodness.

Rituals and laws were created by the ancient kings to guide human nature toward goodness, Hsün-tzu believed. And he strongly upheld the practice of traditional rituals in order to keep desires in check.

Hsün-tzu also believed that all people are endowed with an intellect, and that through consciously redirecting negative impulses toward goodness, people can deliberately improve. In this sense, Hsün-tzu can be viewed as a rationalist—valuing the power of human reason to save us from ourselves. The only possible path to take was to develop conscientious thinking within an organized society. "The mind is the supervisor of the Way" (Watson 1969, 147). Despite all the negative forces that push and pull, people can develop virtue and behave well through a deliberate application of reason.

> *Hsün-tzu said, Heaven does not give up the winter because people dislike cold. Earth does not give up its expanse because people dislike distance. The superior man does not give up good conduct because the inferior man rails against him.* (*Hsün-tzu* in Watson 1969, 98)

Hsün-tzu believed strongly in human culture. Through regulation in a virtuous, positive social system, human beings can become good and live a civilized, happy life. Hsün-tzu was a proponent of all institutions that helped to develop potential.

RECTIFICATION OF NAMES

One contribution Hsün-tzu added to Confucianism was his careful analysis of what was known as rectification of names. This referred to the correct use of language and terminology. Confucius and Mencius both mentioned this problem, but Hsün-tzu developed solutions. Hsün-tzu believed that each name should refer to a specific thing. Confusion arises when the same word is used to describe different and often contrasting objects.

Hsün-tzu recognized that names have intrinsic meaning only when they are given one through association with a particular use or reference. By themselves, names have no correctness of their own. Therefore, human beings could improve their understanding through the correct use of language, especially vocabulary.

Hsün-tzu gave many examples of how names and things relate. Sometimes two things have the same appearance, but are actually different. In this case, they should have different names. By contrast, some things appear different but are actually the same thing at different times. For example, a young person grows old yet is still the same individual throughout. Hsün-tzu believed that if people would use words correctly and clearly, there would be more cooperation and less misunderstandings.

CONFUCIANISM'S SUPPRESSION AND REINTEGRATION

The Ch'in dynasty (221–207 B.C.), with its legalistic dogma, ruthlessly suppressed the individual. Paradoxically, Li Ssu (d. 208 B.C.) chief counselor under the first emperor of Ch'in, and Han Fei-tzu (d. 233 B.C.), a writer who defected to Ch'in, were former students of Hsün-tzu. They reinterpreted state control to mean strict dictatorship by the monarchy, a great loss for China. In the brief period of the Ch'in dynasty, Confucian views were suppressed as well. All books on any differing views were burned. Centralized authority, uniform standardization of laws, currency, and writing contributed to the general unification of China, but it took place through tyranny and opposition. The Ch'in dynasty, as Confucians would have predicted, collapsed fifteen years after it began.

The Han dynasty (206 B.C.–A.D. 220), which followed the Ch'in, was a period during which Confucian ideas were applied by the government. Wen-Ti (179–159 B.C.) ruled unselfishly, putting Confucian values into his policies. He cut the costs of his own administration so that he could reduce the tax burden on the people. He solicited feedback from his subjects and put what he learned to constructive use. Under his rule, the quality of life was high for the everyday citizen. China became more prosperous than it had ever been before. Confucianism worked!

TRADITIONAL CONFUCIAN CLASSICS

Confucian ideas were recast during the Han dynasty to include some of the indigenous ideas of early times. Confucian scholars who grew up during the fourth and third centuries B.C. had been immersed in Taoism, *I Ching*, and Buddhism's cosmological speculations, which offered answers to questions not addressed by Confucius. Now Confucians integrated these ideas with the classical ideas of Confucius and Mencius.

The traditional Confucian classics were called the Five Ching and the Four Shu. The term *Ching* refers to the warp threads of a fabric and their adjustment, denoting what is the true pattern, authoritative and correct. Ching refers to the highest truths and laws upon these subjects. The term *Shu* means writings or books—literally, "the pen speaks."

The Five Ching include the *Book of Changes* (*I Ching*), the *Book of History* (*Shu*), the *Book of Odes* (*Shih*), the *Spring and Autumn Chronicles* (*Ch'un Ch'in*), and the *Book of Rites* (*Li Chi*). Sometimes a group of writings known as the *Record of Music*, the *Yo Chi*, is added as the sixth ching. Confucius's commentary on the *Book of Changes*, the *Ten Wings*, was added as an appendix. Confucius edited the *Li Chi*, largely written by others.

The Four Shu are the books of four philosophers. The *Analects*, as mentioned earlier, is a collection of the sayings of Confucius. The *Great Learning* was written by Ta Hsia, one of Confucius's students. The *Doctrine of the Mean* (*Chung Yung*) was composed by Confucius's grandson Tzse-sze. The *Book of Mencius* includes Mencius's writings.

During the Han, these books were subjected to study and venerated by Confucian scholars. Two books on rituals, *Chou Li* and *I Li*, along with three commentaries on the *Spring and Autumn Annals* (*Ch'un Chiu, Ku Liang Kung*

Liang, and *Tso*—grouped together as one) were added along with the *Classic of Filial Piety*. When combined with the Ching and Shu, the number of books for classical study was thirteen. This collection became the Confucian Canon of the Han dynasty.

TUNG CHUNG-SHU, THE CONFUCIAN UNIFIER

Tung Chung-shu (179–104 B.C.) was a wise Confucian of the Han dynasty. He tempered Hsün-tzu's authoritarianism with Mencius's positive view of human nature, forming an integration of the two theories that was optimistic about human potential within realistic bounds. He combined Confucian views with the prevalent theories of his time, expanding Confucianism to include cosmology. The Neo-Confucians carried his synthesis with other ideas into the modern age. Tung also persuaded the Han emperor, Wu-ti (140–87 B.C.), to accept Confucian values.

Tung was a scholar who devoted himself to study and writing. During one three-year period he was said to be so involved in his work that he did not once look out into his garden. The result of these years was his literary writing, *Luxuriant Dew from the Spring and Summer Annals (Ch'un Ch'io Fan-lu)*.

Tung made a lasting contribution to Chinese culture and to the world by helping to initiate and institute the famous civil service exam, based on Confucian doctrines. The Chinese used this system for nearly two thousand years to test people for governmental positions. The exam was given periodically throughout the country and was open to everyone—nobles and peasants alike. Governmental positions were earned based on the Confucian ideal of virtue and merit. Similar concepts are used today in the West, when people are given jobs based on what they know and do, not just on who they are or who they know.

HUMAN NATURE

Tung's view of human nature synthesized both Mencius and Hsün-tzu's positions together. While Mencius believed human nature was already good,

Tung thought human nature was potentially good, just was not automatically realized. Tung believed that, with a moral and wise government, society could help people fulfill their positive potential for goodness. He felt the Han government could carry out this role.

Tung believed that heaven, earth, and human beings are all related to each other, like the hands and feet are related to the body. He raised the status of human beings by considering people as duplicates of heaven, both physically and mentally. "Heaven gives them birth, earth gives them nourishment, and man gives them perfection" (Fung Yu-lan 1966, 194). How mankind makes perfection real in the world is through rituals and music—culture. Tung believed human society completes heaven. It is an indispensable part of the cosmos.

Unifying Confucianism with Other Views

Tung orchestrated Confucianism with two important ideas of the period: yin-yang theory and the five elements. Tung looked at the universe as made of ten parts: heaven, earth, yin, yang, the five elements (wood, fire, soil, metal, and water), and human beings. People are constantly immersed in yin and yang, like fish live in water. Everything that occurs is a result of yin and yang and their movement. Nothing is static: The only constant is that everything changes. The five elements pass one from the other when, for example, burning wood returns to the soil as ash. The four seasons inevitably move, one to the next, and night always turns to day. The five elements and yin-yang theories were integral to religious Taoism, which was growing in popularity. This would be expressed in the eleventh-century Neo-Confucians.

After the Han dynasty, Confucianism fell out of favor as Buddhism and Taoism spread in popularity throughout China. Confucianism was reintroduced during the T'ang dynasty (618–907), but did not gain momentum until the eleventh-century Neo-Confucian movement.

CHAPTER 5

Neo-Confucianism:
The Great Synthesis

The most valuable things in the world are moral principle and virtue.
—Paraphrased from *Chou Tzu Ch'iian-shu* in Wing-tsit Chan,
A Source Book in Chinese Philosophy

ELEVENTH-CENTURY NEO-CONFUCIANISM

A rebirth of Confucianism, known as Neo-Confucianism, took form in eleventh-century China during the Sung dynasty (960–1279). Most of these Confucians were knowledgeable about Taoism and Buddhism. And rather than oppose them, the Neo-Confucians assimilated these perspectives along with the accepted philosophical beliefs of the day: yin-yang theory and the five elements. Neo-Confucianism took on a broader cosmological orientation like that of Buddhism and Taoism, but remained grounded in the here-and-now world of daily life. The Neo-Confucians synthesized a more complete Confucianism, one that integrated the best qualities of Chinese indigenous philosophies.

Vase with Cover, Nephrite, 1736–1796. San Diego Museum of Art (Gift of Mrs. George D. Pratt) *This vase pictures the eight trigrams along with the yin-yang, integrated into Neo-Confucian thought.*

CHOU TUN-I

Chou Tun-I (1017–1073) was a pioneering Neo-Confucian. He integrated the *I Ching* along with Taoism's theories of yin-yang and the Tao, laying out a number of ideas that became fundamental for Neo-Confucianism.

Chou lived in Tao-Chou, now modern Hunan, and was influenced by Taoism and Zen. He loved all life. He was so adamant about respecting nature just as it was that he never cut the grass outside his window. He even took on the name Lien-hsi after a favorite stream in his area. He taught and deeply influenced the two Cheng brothers, who would later become the fathers of two separate forms of Neo-Confucianism. Buddhism had such an influence on Chou's thinking that the brothers called him "poor Zen fellow" (Chan 1963A, 462). Chou's genius lay in integrating both Buddhist and Taoist ideas while retaining a strong foundation in Confucianism, which helped shape Neo-Confucianism as a unique and influential force in China for nearly a millennium.

Chou took a cosmological view of Confucianism. He created the Diagram of the Supreme Ultimate (Tai-chi Tu) (see diagram), which is also used by the Taoists. He explained that the Great Ultimate always generates yang through movement. When activity reaches its limit, the Great Ultimate generates yin, and everything becomes tranquil. The cycle repeats, continually moving between activity and tranquillity (see Simpkins & Simpkins, *Simple Taoism,* for more details).

The five elements arise from the movement between yin and yang. All come from the Great Ultimate and, in this sense, are mystically unified. "The many are [ultimately] one, and the one is actually differentiated into the many . . . the one and many each has its own correct state of being" (Chan 1963A, 465).

Just as Buddhists strove toward an ideal way of being—to be a buddha— Chou encouraged Neo-Confucians to strive to become sages, the perfect human beings. All people are endowed with intelligence and consciousness and five moral principles in their nature: jen, righteousness, propriety, wisdom, and faithfulness. Sages develop these qualities and learn how to express

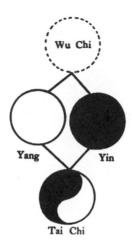

Diagram of the Supreme Ultimate

them in their everyday living. Once these qualities are developed, it is said, the sages will enjoy good fortune. People who violate these principles will have bad luck and misfortune. Like all the Confucians before him, Chou believed that sincerity was the foundation by which the entire process becomes possible.

Becoming a sage meant learning to master oneself. As Chou wrote, "If a man can for one day master himself and return to propriety, all under heaven will return to humanity" (Chan 1963A, 466). Sages could live naturally and act naturally. Because they had developed clarity of mind, their actions would always be correct.

People train to be a sage by learning how to quiet their minds in meditation. With tranquillity, the sage becomes more intelligent and is then able to live according to the moral principles. Chou encouraged his students to learn from their mistakes, to follow the middle way of moderation, and to use teachers when needed.

CHANG TSAI

Chang Tsai (1020–1077), another eleventh-century scholar, helped to steer the course that Neo-Confucianism would take. During his childhood in Ch'ang-an, now Shensi, China, Chang immersed himself in Confucianism, but he became dissatisfied with this philosophy and ventured into Buddhism and Taoism. Eventually, he returned to the Confucian classics, especially the *I Ching* and *The Doctrine of the Mean*. He worked for the government for a time, but was ousted for opposing a reform program, and spent the remainder of his professional years quietly teaching. The Cheng brothers studied under him, adding his influence to their formulation of the two Neo-Confucian schools.

Like Mencius, Chang had definite ideas about developing a fair system for farming. He called it the well field system. A field would be divided into nine plots, with each of eight families owning one plot. The ninth plot was to be farmed together by all and its proceeds given to the government as tax. After he left his governmental work he attempted to set up a well field system with other scholars. Think of how easy tax day would be!

Chang's cosmological theory was different from Chou's, who believed the Great Ultimate evolved into the two forces, yin and yang, which then became the five elements that became all the things in the world, including human beings. For Chang, material force, which he called *chi,* was the same as the Great Ultimate. He considered all else, like yin and yang and the five elements, to simply be aspects of chi. Influenced by Buddhism and Taoism, Chang believed that all material things begin as a great emptiness that manifests as a harmony between activity and tranquillity. All are unified as one, the Way (Tao). Although the universe is One, it manifests in many unique individual ways.

The Great Void [the Tao] cannot but consist of Ch'i; this Ch'i cannot but con-
dense to form all things, and these things cannot but become dispersed so as to
form the Great Void. The perpetuation of these movements in a cycle is
inevitable and thus spontaneous. (Fung Yu-lan 1966, 280)

Like the other Confucians, Chang gave human beings a central role. Heaven and Earth are universal parents. Heaven was Chang's father and Earth his mother. He regarded everything that fills the universe as part of his nature. All people were his brothers and sisters, and all things were his friends. Chang believed that people should love each other and treat everything and everyone as a beloved family member or close friend.

People can live in harmony with the universe by simply leading normal, natural lives, doing their duty as members of society and the world. Everything has principle that should be investigated as deeply as possible. If we fail to do so, Chang said, we would remain in a dream our whole life and, as a result, not awaken to become the true sages we can be.

THE CHENG BROTHERS

The Cheng brothers, Cheng-Hao (1032–1085) and Cheng-I (1033–1108), were students of Chou Tun-I and were nephews of Chang Tsai. Cheng-I believed the principle of natural law governs all things from within, giving pattern to life's creations. He founded the rational school of Neo-Confucianism, the School of Principle. Cheng-I, the younger brother, who outlived his older brother by twenty-two years, was critical of the government and so lost favor for one hundred years! His school was brought to full flower by Chu Hsi. This philosophy is called the Cheng-Chu School.

Cheng-Hao dreamed of a higher universal mind unifying all things and developed a metaphysics of oneness that led to the idealistic school of Neo-Confucianism. His teachings were developed by Lu Chiu-yuan (1139–1193) and later evolved by Wang Yang-ming. This became the Lu-Wang School, also known as the School of Mind.

Cheng-Hao had a very different temperament from his brother, Cheng-I. Cheng-I was stern, critical, and prone to strongly assert his opinion; Cheng-Hao was gentle, warm, agreeable, and tolerant. These personality differences may have led to their differing emphases in their interpretations of Confucianism, although the brothers did not consider themselves as far apart on their ideas as history has remembered them.

Probably because of these strong differences in personality, the two brothers led very different lives. Cheng-Hao gained acceptance of his ideas, holding a number of positions, including magistrate. Emperor Shen-tsung accepted many of his recommendations, although after he opposed a radical reform movement, Cheng-Hao was demoted for several years. Finally, he was offered a new position, but died before he could take office.

Cheng-I was as intelligent as his brother, but he lacked his brother's social graces, particularly tact and charm. He boldly proclaimed his beliefs and had no qualms about criticizing others, including the government. As a result, he developed bitter enemies in high places. Eventually, as Confucianism would predict, he lost the position he had been given, his teachings were prohibited, his land was confiscated, his books were burned, and he was banished to another province. Although he was pardoned in 1106, he died soon after.

The main difference between the theories of the brothers was that Cheng-Hao focused on the cultivation of one's own mind whereas Cheng-I always tempered self-cultivation with learning and knowledge. Cheng-I believed that principle is in all things and that studying is the pathway to understanding these principles. Applying yourself sincerely to learning is primary because everything, from the very smallest to the most expansive, contains principle. The more you study, the more you come to understand principle.

Cheng-Hao felt that he had made his most important breakthroughs by turning his attention inward, so he believed that developing inwardly was more important. He sought to be calm and impartial. When people can develop serious and sincere concentration they will come to recognize the unity of all things. Cheng-Hao stated that principle and the mind are one.

CHAPTER 6

Masters of Neo-Confucianism: Chu Hsi and Wang Yang-ming

In saying that altruism is Love, altruism must not be regarded as parallel to Love. Altruism is simply the absence of selfishness; when there is no selfishness Love has free course.
—Chu Hsi

CHU HSI

Chu Hsi (1130–1200), a student of Cheng-I, was the leading scholar of the rational school of Neo-Confucianism and was one of the most influential and important Neo-Confucians. His prolific writings and commentaries on the classics helped Confucianism gain wide acceptance long after his death.

Chu Hsi was born into an intellectual family. He studied both Buddhism and Taoism, and later returned to Confucianism. His doctrines included aspects of these theories. He passed his advanced scholar degree, similar to a

Ph.D., at the age of eighteen, when most people did not complete their degree until they were thirty. Chu Hsi began his career at a young age with his first official post as a registrar in Fukien Province from 1151 to 1158. He was always considered an honest and zealous officer.

Public office, however, was not his true calling. He withdrew from governmental work for twenty years, during which time he was extremely productive and creative. He established a teaching academy while also carrying on voluminous correspondence with other intellectuals, writing commentaries on the classics, and continuing his own education.

Finally, in 1182, Chu Hsi accepted another post—to administer the granaries in Chekiang. Through his efforts, he relieved a famine and rid the department of a number of corrupt officials. This action brought a counterattack, so he withdrew again from political involvement. Later in life, Chu Hsi accepted a position under the Emperor Kuang and continued under the emperor's son, but again became caught up in the political intrigues of an ambitious minister. Chu Hsi died unrecognized, without knowing the enormous impact his work would one day have on China.

LI RULES SUPREME

Chu Hsi stepped through Alice's looking glass, and the Confucian world as we know it was turned inside out forever by his Neo-Confucian theory. After the Tao was fully accepted and embraced, brought from heaven into humanity, the world of objective reality was no longer conceived of as simply a world of objects. Instead, the world was composed of energy taking form as matter, orchestrated by principle. As we follow the path shown us by Chu Hsi, we find principle expressed everywhere.

Ideal patterns of form are embodied in real, actual things. This example illustrates: The purpose of an airplane is to fly. Its design enables it to do so. A passenger plane has an individual *li* that is different from that of a stealth fighter plane. A jumbo passenger jet would not make a good stealth fighter plane. Each type of plane has its own individual li as well as having the ideal li of airplanes in general, a function of ultimate li.

Actual flying, as it takes place, is the action but not the li. The action, however, is a function of li and thus depends on it. So, one seeks the principle to correctly guide action. Principle can be found in action, but it does not derive from action.

In Chu Hsi's theory, li as principle is inherent in matter, not separable from it. His theory states that li produces substance, which he called chi. Substance cannot exist without li, but li does not require substance. Actual expression in the world is chi, whereas the potential in ideal form is li.

Principle is inherent in more than just substance. Principle is inherent in social matters as well. Everything we do should be guided by principle. "Principle is the transcendent Tao and is the root which produces all things" (Wittenborn 1991, 32).

The Tao of Heaven, Tao of Earth, and Tao of Man all follow the universal Tao, bringing out its nature by the inner principle. Li is preeminent but not supreme. It creates substance but is not the ruler. Mind is. "Mind embraces or possesses all principles, and all principles are complete within the mind" (Wittenborn 1991, 32). Chu Hsi stated that without mind, principle would have nowhere to reside.

When principle is understood by the mind, it becomes our human nature. Human nature and feelings are both included in mind. The inner essence of humanity's principle is jen, human-heartedness and benevolence. The realization in actuality of human nature's true pattern is unique for each individual.

Sages in Chu Hsi's system should therefore seek to perfect themselves by sincerely extending their knowledge, accomplished by investigating combined with analytically seeking the true nature within things. Quiet sitting, a special form of meditation, combined with focused concentration can help to bring this comprehensive understanding to fruition. Investigation of things, with an emphasis on study, begins with your own clear, focused mind (for more on meditation, see Chapter 11).

Like Mencius, Chu Hsi believed that human nature is inherently good, endowed from heaven. Sincere social action in accord with virtues of love, righteousness, propriety, and wisdom is the Tao of human interaction. The point of learning and the moral education that Chu Hsi advocated is to clear away the misunderstanding and ignorance that prevents our innate good nature from shining through. Everyday life grants the circumstances, the loom on which to weave the threads of virtue into the beautiful cloth of our life's destiny.

Thus, Chu Hsi was very aware of the importance of focus and concentration, allowing the inner nature to be actualized in sincere, genuine being.

Master Chu said: If you wish to respond to things you should first make a thorough investigation of the principles. And if you wish to thoroughly investigate the principles, then you must cultivate the fundamentals of the mind. Only by keeping it tranquil and clear will you be able to examine the most minute points and analyze the most disordered material without the least error. (Wittenborn 1991, 97)

LOVE

The nature of mind is love, jen. Absolute, heavenly Tao is prior to ethics, prior to love, and prior to righteousness. The Tao of humanity *is* love in relationship. No separation exists. "The term 'Love' is not derived from altruism, but from man; hence the statement, 'It is when altruism as embodied in man is Love'" (Bruce 1922, 346).

Tao *is* sincerity and value. And the source of value is *in* nature, not apart from it. Tao refers to the mystical nature common to all, and thus, though the description of it seems to distinguish between the individual manifestation and the transcendental essence, no distinction is necessary. Tao is both—a unified essence. The root and its fruit are of one essential nature, the same plant. The fruit cannot happen without contact with its root, in everyday life.

Human relationships are intimately linked to Tao, love, sincerity, and law. All are part of the true nature, not separate or empty. All should be respected and sincerely engaged in.

Chu Hsi encourages us to be positive in order to be correct and true to reality. Our thoughts and actions matter. What we do and how we treat others in our daily lives matters deeply. Chu Hsi returns our focus to our personal, everyday life, to live and relate to others with sincere and serious intensity. We should play our parts in the fabric of social life with enthusiasm and love, as an intrinsic part of enlightened living.

LU-WANG SCHOOL

The line of the Lu-Wang School, or School of Mind, began with Cheng-Hao's interpretation of Confucianism, continued with Lu Chiu-yuan (1139–1193), and extended with Wang Yang-ming (1472–1529).

Lu Chiu-yuan, also known as Lu Hsiang-shan, was a native of Kiongsi Province. He differed with Chu Hsi publicly about some concepts, but privately they were friends. This school of Neo-Confucianism believed sudden enlightenment was possible, which was contrary to the gradual cultivation and study put forth by Chu Hsi's school. In an ancient text that explained the concepts of *yu* and *chou*, Lu read that yu refers to the directions, points of the compass combined with above and below, and that chou refers to past, present, and future objects. Lu experienced a sudden enlightenment from these concepts. He realized that "All affairs within the universe come within the scope of my duty; the scope of my duty includes all affairs within the universe" (Fung Yu-lan 1966, 33).

Later, Lu enlarged on his insight: "The universe is my mind; my mind is the universe" (Fung Yu-lan 1966, 36). To Lu, li was not the essence within, nature. Li was Mind. And all is mind.

WANG YANG-MING

Everything from ruler, minister, husband, wife, and friends to mountains, rivers, spiritual beings, birds, animals, and plants should be truly loved in order to realize my humanity that forms one body with them, and then my clear character will be completely manifested, and I will really form one body with Heaven, Earth, and the myriad things. (Wang in Chan 1963B, 273)

Wang believed in oneness of knowledge and action and instantaneous enlightenment, but he did not begin his career thinking this way. During his early years, he attempted to follow Chu Hsi's idea of investigating the principle of things. Along with a friend, Wang sat in front of some bamboo and earnestly tried to investigate their principles. Unable to discover any, his friend gave up after three days. Wang finally stopped after seven. Disillusioned with Confucianism, Wang looked into Taoism for some years, but returned to Confucianism, passing the civil service exams and later pursuing a career as a Confucian scholar and official.

Wang lived in a time of corruption in government. The emperor was a playboy who rode horses and played, leaving the business of politics for others to run for him. This led to a poorly run government, economic crisis, and widespread lawlessness, an excellent opportunity for an honorable man.

WANG'S IDEAS

Wang believed that knowledge implies action, and action implies knowledge. He did not think they could be separated. If the people understood knowledge, Wang believed that they would act accordingly. No obstruction, no separation was possible. Deep, intensive study results in a clear understanding of how to act in relation to the object of knowledge. Action is inevitable for the sincere person, true to reality. Understanding, to Wang, implies actually doing what you ought to do; potential must become actualized.

Wang believed that each person has innate knowledge and innate ability—the foundation of intelligence, virtue, and successful action. Comprehension comes from these qualities. Originally, the mind is empty of content but filled with innate understanding. Innate knowledge is identical to the intuitive wisdom of Zen, but it needs active expression to evolve and refine one's life. "Innate knowledge is the original substance of the mind. It is what I have just referred to as that which is always shining" (Wang in Chan 1963B, 132).

Wang believed that Cheng-I and Chu Hsi's view that mind has substance and function should be modified. Mind has these aspects, revealed in activity as function and in tranquillity as substance, but essentially they are one.

> *Activity and tranquillity are one. If it is in accord with the Principle of Nature, the mind that is empty and tranquil at midnight will be the same mind that responds to events and deals with affairs now. (Wang in Chan 1963B, 203)*

Truth is truth and The Way is the Way, wherever found. Partisan positions are untrue to the Way. Wang encouraged his students to respect truth and wisdom whenever found.

Since the inner nature of mind is primary, all things follow from this. No part is unrelated to the whole. Therefore, either quiet sitting or dynamic activity can all be expressions of Confucian principle. Both are the Way.

Innate knowledge and true insight in Wang are fundamental and linked together as one. Innate knowledge is not internal, not external. It involves both. The sage remains in the world of objects, events, and people without concern for how to accomplish objectives or what exact rules of action to follow. The rules follow the reality as it unfolds. Imitation was hollow to Wang; external guides or criteria were mere illusion.

Each reality is complete and integrated. The pattern that emerges must be followed. The whole determines its parts as needed. We are all part of the whole and should play our parts faithfully. Practice completes enlightenment. Practice makes perfect becomes practice is perfection.

Innate knowledge guides the investigation of things, which extends knowledge further, leading to a sincere will carried out in actual practice. Wang encouraged his students to seek equilibrium by following principle in nature, mastering themselves in the midst of activity rather than retiring to meditate in quiet and solitude. Wang taught his students to observe themselves and correct their faults by using appropriate methods: calming with meditation or going with the flow.

If during the day one feels work becoming annoying, one should sit in meditation. But if one feels lazy and not inclined to read, then he should go ahead and read. To do this is like applying medicine according to the disease. (Chan 1963B, 26)

Wang taught to the individual's intellectual abilities, believing that some students could comprehend immediately, without moral guidance, while others need rules of conduct to follow. Wang's teaching included both, so that all could follow principle according to their natural abilities, habits, and efforts at correct conduct.

Wang's open-minded philosophy inspired a wide spectrum of people. From imperialist administrators to revolutionary leaders, all claimed him as their source. The fact that such diverse people drew from him shows the broad and comprehensive nature of his approach.

PART II

Confucian Themes

What can we believe in
When faced with life's doubts
When lost in the moments
That swirl all about
We must open our hearts
To endure and transcend
Then currents of Fate
Become paths we can wend
—C. Alexander Simpkins

Confucian themes revolve around how to live and be in relationships. Everyday life is the focus. Making it the best it can be is the goal. Confucius shows us ways to cope and ways to evolve so we can awaken the inner core of wisdom, the untapped potential within, and become a sage.

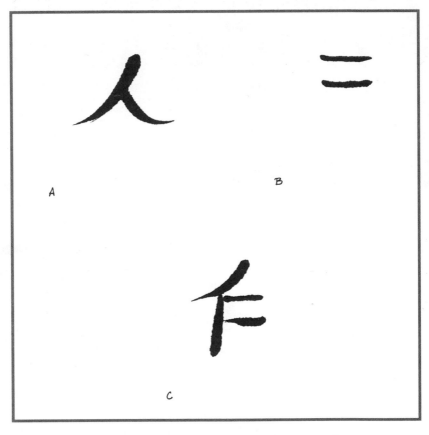

**Humanity (A) combines with Relationship (B) to form Jen (C)
(Calligraphy)**

CHAPTER 7

Jen: Begin with Benevolence

In so far as a thing is in harmony with our nature, it is necessarily good.
—Spinoza

Confucius searched through space and time, seeking in the wellspring of harmony the core of virtue. His vision revealed a timeless truth, resonating with the rhythms of the human heart—jen.

"Jen is all embracing, not a virtue among others, but the soul of all virtues" (Jaspers 1962, 50). Jen is benevolence, agape, expressing the Tao of humanity. Jen is the ultimate, the fountainhead from which all virtues flow: wisdom, love, compassion, equality. Jen is the central source of virtue, manifested as *yi*, righteousness. The mean, the principle of central harmony, is founded in jen; it transcends any other virtue or quality. It is fundamental to all qualities, the basis of virtue. Morality begins with love.

Jen refers to humankind, human nature itself, and always includes others. Jen's moral implications imply relationship. The ideogram for jen also includes the ideogram for "two," implying that dialogue and communication are part of jen. To be is to be in relationship. The nature of humanity is jen.

> To find the central clue to our moral being which unites us to the universal order (or to attain central harmony), that indeed is the highest human attainment. For a long time people have seldom been capable of it. (Yutang 1994, 186)

JEN IS ALREADY THERE

> A man is the facade of a temple wherein all wisdom and all good abide.
> —Ralph Waldo Emerson

Confucius and Mencius believed human nature is intrinsically good, though human conduct could be negative. A person may have negative experiences and learnings throughout life, and these negative experiences may prevent the expression and actualization of positive potential. Confucius had faith in human nature, whether it was actualized in any particular expression or not. Classical Confucianism was optimistic. People have almost infinite untapped resources for goodness within. Even Hsün-tzu believed that with personal effort and learning from the culture, people can become good. The sage does nothing more than bring out in others what is already there in latent form.

Jen is a quality unique to people that distinguishes us from animals. Animals are not capable of this fundamentally human quality, with its moral implications. Goodness derives from human loving kindness.

Confucius offers a solution to the age-old dilemma, how to reach the highest potential in human functioning, to cope with the base animal nature presumed to be part of our being. His solution is to fully embrace and live the human qualities already present within our nature, setting us naturally apart from and above the animal instincts. Therefore, *be* jen, *live* according to jen, and express and evolve your *human* nature to its highest potential.

LIVING WITH JEN

To live according to jen means to live in synchrony and harmony with the loving benevolence within. Mencius said that the benevolent person has no enemies. Jen requires benevolence that is altruistic, sincere, and sympathetic toward others. As Mencius said, "The doctrine of our master is to be true to the principles of our nature and the benevolent exercise of them to others—this and nothing more" (*Analects* 4–7, in Legge 1971, 170).

All-embracing love for our own family is primary. Filial piety, the cornerstone of Chinese culture, is an expression of jen in the family. When we treat our family with jen we set benevolence in motion, enhancing our family, our community, our country, and ultimately the whole world in loving kindness. As Emerson pointed out, "We have a great deal more kindness than is ever spoken" (Emerson 1926, 137).

Not only is jen basic to Confucius's thought, but all later Confucians included jen as fundamental to their system. Later, the Neo-Confucians redefined jen, developing a complex concept of human nature at One with the universe. Jen is humanity's positive contribution to the cosmos as it passes through its ceaseless transformations.

CHUNG, SHU, AND THE SILVER RULE

Jen has two related polar facets of practice in action—*chung* and *shu*—that guide us in what we should and should not do. Chung, the mean, is positive and clear. Similar to the golden rule, chung guides conduct in active terms, telling us to treat others well according to the true standard, with benevolence, to develop a sense of righteousness, what should be done according to life's role relationships and station in life. Treat others with empathy, conscientiously. Chung is active, positive, and decisive: to behave according to benevolent love and respect, unconditionally and sincerely. The standard of judgment, to choose and determine what you should do, is within your own self, at one with your nature. Choices of how to treat parents, family, or others in relationship are made according to this.

The silver rule is the yin pole of jen, the receptive, the guide to conduct. The silver rule, shu, means to live by altruism, the essence of the golden rule, without necessarily expecting its reciprocal. Do not do to others as you would not have them do to you.

> *The silver rule, with its interactive quality, was one of the most important*
> *principles to Confucius. Confucius explained this in a conversation:*
> *Confucius said, "Ah Ts'an, there is a central principle that runs through all*
> *my teachings."*
> *"Yes," said Tseng-tse.*
> *When Confucius left, the disciples asked Tseng-tse what he meant,*
> *and Tseng-tse replied, "It is just the principle of reciprocity (or shu)."*
> *(Yutang 1994, 185)*

The silver rule is similar to the golden rule we know so well, but it is expressed as a prohibition, a restraint; *not* to treat others as you would *not* want to be treated. You become the reference point for the standard of conduct to judge by. The source is within. Response from others is not your criterion; your personal action should not depend on the recognition of others. Each situation is an opportunity to do the correct thing for itself, to behave appropriately. If others do not, then even more are you offered a challenging opportunity to behave well. This is the Tao of human relationship, constant and true.

Adhere to the center, to the essence: The Tao of humanity is expressed as benevolence and selfless love. The criterion of truth is not dependent on outer circumstance or transitory interactions with ungrateful others. The source of correct, sincere truth and goodness is in each person's humanity, the heart.

Others may not always reciprocate; others may even attempt injustices. Correct action is not dependent on response. Correct action is complete in and of itself. You do it to do it because it is right.

ACCEPTING MING

Destiny, *ming*, flows from living with jen. Do things because it is correct to do them, not for results. If there are no results, it is not important. If there are results, it is not important either. All that matters is that the action itself is done. Ming takes place. We cannot know all the effects or consequences. Like ripples from a stone thrown into a pond, or a dandelion blown in the wind, the effects of our actions drift and settle to evolve in ways we cannot possibly imagine or predict, though we can sometimes approximate. Too many variables, too many other forces influence the flowering of our actions. Therefore, we must select the action for itself, to be correct and true, and not for recognition or results. Then we cannot fail, and we have no worry or tension about how things may turn out. The sage is calm and serene while others, less wise, are constantly agitated and worried. In giving ourselves fully to the moment, sincerely allowing ourselves to be our best selves, we will usually succeed. We may not see past this moment. But beyond the dim horizon of our personal vision, destiny is taking form.

Li: Principle (Calligraphy)

CHAPTER 8

Li and Wen: Central Harmony Is the Way

As the curtain parts gently
We glimpse forms through its folds
—C. Alexander Simpkins

LI: THE FUNDAMENTAL PRINCIPLE

Li is a fundamental virtue—that is, form or principle. It is expressed as propriety, conduct, forms of relationship, and action. Li includes the rituals, customs, and patterns of life. Chu Hsi believed that li and chi are the basis of all that is. Li has been interpreted in many ways, but its meaning always returns to the essence of form, the form within.

Confucians revere this essence within essence, the form of form itself, the pattern of pattern. American philosopher Ralph Waldo Emerson (1803–1882) understood the concept of trueness to li, although he did not call it that. He eulogized the inner principle in his transcendental philosophy.

By degrees we may come to know the primitive sense of the permanent objects of nature, so that the world shall be to us an open book, and every form significant of its hidden life and final cause.
(Emerson 1926, 257)

Form precedes essence, so being true to form brings you closer to the true essence. In Zen, form is emptiness, emptiness is form. In Confucianism, form is the ultimate. Form is principle and principle is form. Both philosophies view forms as symbolic of true wisdom, of enlightened perception. Everyday life is truly enlightening!

In our Western tradition we take for granted that material objects are distinct, but thay may also belong to a group, category, or class. Philosopher Bertrand Russell (1872–1970) developed a theory, known as the Russell-Whitehead paradox, that helps provide conceptual clarity concerning li. An object is a member of a class, but it is not the class itself. If one confuses them, a paradox results. For example, a Windsor chair is a kind of chair, just as a Morris chair is a kind of chair. But not all chairs are Colonial-style chairs, Morris chairs, or Windsor chairs. These individual *kinds* of chairs are not actually the universal class of chairs. The universal class of chairs transcends its individual members.

Similarly, the universal pattern of chair (li) is more than its expression as any one particular style or type. Chairs have an ordering principle, a pattern or template of their being, which gives them their character—their chairness, so to speak. A chair is possible due to the ingenious thought someone had of creating a thing to sit on: a chair. The principle of chairs makes individual chairs in our world possible. Each chair embodies this principle, but the principle is not limited to any one chair.

Li Is in This World

In social situations, li is the spirit within that gives meaning or makes meaning possible.

> *It is not words only that are emblematic, it is things that are emblematic.*
> *Every natural fact is a symbol of a spiritual fact. Every appearance in nature*
> *corresponds to some state of the mind, and that state of the mind can only*
> *be described by presenting that appearance as its picture.*
> *(Emerson in Spiller 1965, 194)*

Plato viewed this material world as only the shadow of the ideal world of form. This was pointed out in his famous parable of the cave, in which people were chained in a cave watching shadows on the wall, mistaking them for reality. Western philosophical traditions separate ideal from real. Confucians do not; they relate them together. Confucians teach that the forms of the actual objects in this world are intimately linked to and made possible by the world of form itself. Form precedes, essence follows. Form is expressed in the actual forms of this world, not as an ideal transcendent to them. Li is here and now.

Our human nature is not outside us or beyond us. Li is not outside or beyond this world either. Custom, ritual, and tradition all embody li, but li is not limited to any particular form, custom, or tradition. Li is the spirit of customs, rituals, or traditions themselves. The scholar should study them to learn the transcendent essence through its expression. The North Star is north, but north is more than just the North Star. The direction of north transcends its expression in the North Star, but it is also not apart from it. We can always find the direction of north by finding the North Star.

Therefore, study of the classics, followed by respectful participation in the correct rituals, customs, and traditions, leads to enlightened understanding.

Investigating the nature of things helps the sincere seeker grasp the particular li within, which can lead to li itself. Confucius researched and studied the actual customs, rituals, and traditions of the Chou dynasty and included them in the *Book of Rites* (*Li Chi*). Li of social customs have been followed carefully by all true Confucian scholars since the Master, Confucius himself. Over time, elaborate codes of conduct evolved, but the intent of the Master's teaching was to show reverence to the process, to engage intelligently in the activity itself, not to mindlessly follow the transitory outer form that embodies it.

The Montessori learning method teaches the student to discover abstract principles through concrete activities. For example, the concept of number is taught through counting and sorting objects such as beads into groups. The concept of shape is taught through manipulating particular shaped objects. First, the child learns to discern relationships between specific objects in the actual world. Then, after the child recognizes the principle within, other applications of the relationship become evident. The teacher facilitates this evolution of the mind in part through sensitivity to the transcendent level of understanding as it develops in the child. The Confucian method of learning li through study is similar but goes farther than conceptual abstractions. Correct comprehension of li leads to yi, the oughtness or requiredness of things. Yi leads to moral character.

From Principle to Practice

Abraham Maslow, one of the founders of humanistic psychology, taught that facts have implications. True scholarly learning can result in true wisdom in action. *Is* leads to *ought*; *thought* leads to *action*.

Li becomes manifest as forms of relationship in society. The principle of li in human nature helps determine good and bad, right and wrong in conduct. Filial piety and affection is a direct consequence of li embodied in human relationships. Conduct that strengthens loving and respectful bonds in friendships and families promotes social harmony in general, enhancing the community, which in turn enhances the whole country. Human-heartedness is the ground for all the other virtues. Concern for correct patterns of conduct derives from and expresses jen. The sage is one with these qualities. The wellspring of value itself is inner essence.

WEN: CULTURE AND THE ARTS

Li and wen are often viewed in combination. Li helps channel impulses, giving us self-control through the practice of set rituals and rites. Involvement in the arts, wen, uplifts and expands our spirit. When combined with li, wen helps to cultivate harmony and promote virtue. As Confucius said, "The gentleman with his studies is broadened by culture and yet restrained by the requirements of ritual. Surely he cannot overstep the mark" (*Analects* 6–25, in Legge 1970, 193).

Confucius had a great love for the arts, viewing them as having one of the highest influences on human beings. The arts referred to as wen include music, fine art, poetry, architecture—all the aesthetic, cultured qualities of human creation.

Art has the power to free the soul and elevate humanity to be its best. Confucius's love and respect for art came from recognizing the strong positive effect it has on people. For example, if you have ever stood before the Statue of Liberty, visited the Louvre, looked at a portrait painted by Rembrandt, or listened to a Beethoven symphony, you probably felt uplifted. Your spirit was ennobled as you allowed yourself to experience it deeply and sensitively. Art is an important aspect of human culture and we should involve ourselves with it.

> *Each piece of art affects our emotions in certain ways. Confucius explained: By poetry the mind is aroused; from music the finish is received. The odes stimulate the mind. They induce self-contemplation. They teach the art of sensibility. They help to restrain resentment. (Smith 1991, 179)*

One writer noted that music does for time as architecture does for space (Dawson 1981, 36). Architecture is the music of space; music gives form and pattern to time. Each offers a dimension of experience that influences us. Confucians believe that when art is well developed, it can bring about harmony that affects everyone.

WEN AFFECTS EMOTIONS

People are in equilibrium before their emotions arise. But once moved by a feeling, the equilibrium is disturbed. Emotions can take us in many directions. The correct kind of art can enhance emotions along a positive path. Li tends to direct and channel emotions. In combination, li and wen help us find harmony in the mean.

If equilibrium is the root from which all our actions grow, harmony is the path we should follow. By the balancing of li and wen, we can express our emotions freely while keeping them from being uncontrolled.

CHAPTER 9

Chung: Tao Is Found in the Mean

Virtue, then, is a state of character concerned with choice, lying in a mean, i.e., the mean relative to us, this being determined by a rational principle, and by that principle by which the man of practical wisdom would determine it.
—Aristotle

THE TAO OF HUMANITY

Confucianism, like the other Eastern philosophies, looks to the Tao for the source of wisdom. But Confucianism does not have the same emphasis as Taoism. In Taoism, people seek to become unified with a mysterious, unnameable spirit that permeates all things and yet is always beyond them. Confucians refer to this as the Tao of Heaven. By contrast, Confucians seek unity with Tao in their interactions with other people, and refer to this as the Tao of Humanity. Tao is not apart from humanity; it is sought in relationships.

**Chung: The Mean, The
Center (Calligraphy)**

In China, Confucianism and Taoism were often practiced together. Since they have different spheres, they complement and supplement each other.

Confucians unify with Tao in day-to-day interactions with others. As Confucius said in the *Analects*, the Way does not make human beings great. Instead, human beings make the Way (Tao) great. Confucius told his students that if the Way seemed foreign or apart from their human consciousness, it was not the Way.

Confucius used an apt illustration from the *Book of Odes* to explain the Tao of humanity.

> *We carve an ax handle.*
> *With the use of another ax handle.*
> *The pattern is not far off.*

In order to make one ax handle, the craftsman uses another ax, grasping it by the handle. Our own humanness, including our mind, emotions, and capacity to act, is the tool we must use to find and stay on the path. It is not outside or beyond us.

Human nature at its best is the source, the standard by which to measure all things. We are born with everything we need to become wise. "What Heaven has disposed and sealed is called the inborn nature" (*Doctrine of the Mean*. trans. by Pound 1951, 99). The perfection of the Way is already within, ready and waiting to be actualized. "The realization of this nature is called the process [Tao]" (*Doctrine of the Mean*, in Pound 1951, 99).

Neo-Confucian Chu Hsi developed this principle even further in his commentary on the *Doctrine of the Mean*. He said, "The components, the bones of things, the materials, are implicit and prepared in us, abundant and inseparable from us" (Pound 1951, 99).

Since our capacities are already given in our human-heartedness, our jen, then Tao is open to everyone willing to recognize, accept, and live according to their nature. Staying on this path takes a concerted effort, but it can be done. We must turn away from the negative influences that inevitably come along in life to divert us from who we really are, at our core. Confucius and Mencius sound like modern thinkers when they stated repeatedly that anyone, no matter what their background or ability, could become a sage by truly living out the positive humanity that is already there: "What kind of man was Shun? [The sage king of ancient China.] What kind of man am I? He who exerts himself will also become such as he was" (Mencius in Legge 1970, 235).

The Tao brings all Confucian virtues together when we live them. In being benevolent, honorable, and sincere, we develop our humanity to the fullest, cultivating ourselves as Confucius encouraged. Then we find ourselves naturally doing the right thing and being courageous enough to carry out our convictions with integrity.

THE MEAN IS OUR STANDARD

We can use standards derived from what the Confucians call chung, the mean, to guide us on our path. The mean is the center, the balance point, like a sixth sense within our human nature. Chung is the active, the positive, pointing the Way. Confucius and Mencius stated that fully developed human nature is the standard, the inner try square for trueness, the compass to find direction to steer by on our voyage through life.

When trying to draw a perfect circle, we use a compass. The point of the compass arm becomes the center, the anchor around which the circle is drawn. The circle can be any size, but it will always be a circle, perfectly round. The center point is the reference for any size or number of circles that can emerge.

Similarly, the mean is the center of the personality, the alignment standard for self-cultivation. The mean is within, an inner reference point. For example, although the sage ruler was supposed to set the standard for his people, the leader's standard is within. From the ruler of the land down to the most humble peasant, all have the standard for conduct in their own center: benevolent human nature. When you are centered you are clear.

Confucian theory is reflected in how our brains work. When an on-center type of neuron in the brain is stimulated, it fires at the center. These on-center detectors, as neuropsychologists call them, give us an experience of our environment. For example, when a light is flashed, we see it. When the stimulus is over, the neuron activates off-center to stop the response, bringing about inhibition. A centering process is built into our biological nature. We perceive clearly through being on-center or off-center.

The mean is the moderating center between extremes. Confucius did not tell us exactly what the center point of interaction should be. Instead, he advised his students what not to do to get there: Do not be too extreme. The farther away you get from the center, the more difficult it is to find the mean. Confucius and Mencius advised people not to fulfill every desire, yet they should not deprive themselves completely either. In the balance between we discover wisdom.

Confucius encouraged his students to think, perceive, and learn for themselves. Each person discovers for himself the balance point within. In everything we do and feel there is a correct center with which to align ourselves. The center point varies, of course, from person to person and situation to situation. For example, the emotions we feel and express when watching an adventure movie or reading an uplifting, inspiring book may be different from the feelings we have during a serious meeting at work. Yet each situation has its correct balance for us, appropriate and centered.

The center point may seem elusive, but you have everything you need to discover it for yourself. Confucius explained with a metaphor. We all know how to eat and drink, he said, but how many people can truly taste flavors? Discovering the mean develops from sensitivity, concentration, and careful thought about the principle within all things. People are sometimes too quick to respond, "I got it, I already know!" Then they rush forward without thinking and end up way off-center. Confucians ask us to slow down and, step-by-step, to search deeply to develop our knowledge. Eventually, we will find the mean.

STAYING WITH THE MEAN

The challenge is not to leave the center. When we deviate from the mean, we lose the Tao and face difficulty.

> *The Master said, "This was the manner of Hui:—he made choice of the Mean, and whenever he got hold of what was good, he clasped it firmly, as if wearing it on his breast, and did not lose it." (Doctrine of the Mean,* in Legge 1971, 389)

Confucius is not advising that we cannot try new or different things or be experimental. What is important, no matter what you are doing, is to do it from the point of reference of your center. Do not anchor your perception away from the center. Just as the compass can help you draw any size circle you want, so too you can explore anything you are interested in, so long as you always keep the mean, your center, as your source.

The fully developed sage is not thrown off-center by inevitable difficulties of life. We have all experienced times when everything seems to go wrong as life presents one hardship after another. The sage pays attention to the environment, to what is happening, and makes the best choices to deal with each challenge. The unenlightened person rushes ahead without even noticing. Center yourself in the constant, the invariable—your humanity, jen, which is always there to guide you in the right direction. Then you can make correct decisions and cope with adversity.

CHAPTER 10

Chün-tzu: The Good and Noble Person

Whatever the world may say or do, my part is to remain an
emerald and to keep my color true.
—Marcus Aurelius

Confucians have described a path to perfection within, a Way to fully develop human potential. Just as a Buddhist strives to become a bodhisattva, a wise and compassionate helper of society, Confucians become a *Chu-tse*, a sage. Sagehood is the full flowering of human beings—humanity at its best. Chu-tse has been translated in various ways, each emphasizing an important aspect of sagehood: the true person, the wise person, and the noble person.

THE TRUE PERSON

The sage is a true person, which means being sincere and true to inner nature. Confucius believed sincerity comes first. He said, "Hold faithfulness

Sage Ruler (Calligraphy)

and sincerity as first principles" (*Analects* 1-8-2, in Legge 1971, 141). No one walks the path to sagehood without sincerity.

All people make mistakes, but few have the humility to admit when they are at fault and correct their action. Confucius recognized one student above the others, not just because he was able to take responsibility for his faults, but because he was willing to face his errors; he never made the same mistake twice. Confucius demands humility and honesty, especially when no one else is there to enforce discipline or provide correction. The archer who misses the mark finds fault in his own technique rather than blame the target. Similarly, sincere seekers must be willing to doubt and question their technique when things go wrong. We develop our potential by learning as we journey along the path. In time, we can all come to embody the best that humanity can be.

Human nature is basically good. Expressing the positive in human nature is a choice given on life's journey. Developing yourself fully on the Confucian path means that you not only learn to value the innate goodness within, but that you also come to love living in accord with it. Then you are on the correct path, the benevolent and human-hearted path. As Confucius said,

> *Better than one who knows what is right is one who is fond of what is right; and better than one who is fond of what is right is one who delights in what is right.* (Giles 1998, 60)

Confucius believed that when people embrace virtue and make it a constant companion, life works out. A plant with the potential to flower, cared for in good soil, with adequate sunlight, just the right amount of water, given correct nutrients, will grow into a beautiful, healthy flowering plant for all to enjoy. Similarly, each of us can develop completely, when appropriately nourished by living according to correct conditions, to become a highly functioning person. We only use five to ten percent of our potential. Much more awaits us if we learn to access the rest.

Living virtuously develops stronger personality. Then we can discern what we should do, our life's tasks, and perform correct actions accordingly. True persons, true to the highest within them, have the courage to do the right thing.

Other people may also be affected in a positive way by the inner strength of the sage. The good qualities that begin within the individual generalize to help others. "The man of moral virtue [jen], wishing to stand firm himself, will lend firmness unto others" (Giles 1998, 63).

THE WISE PERSON

Confucius believed in fulfilling the roles we play in life, whatever they may be. The prince should be a prince, the minister a minister, the father a father, and the son a son (paraphrased from *Analects* 12-11, in Legge 1971, 256). If we are to develop ourselves like the sages, we need to learn to live wisely, to incorporate the best that knowledge has to offer.

Being fully involved in our lives means learning all about the roles we play, so that we can perform correctly. For example, if you are a parent, be a parent—fully. Do not be a parent only on weekdays and run away on weekends to be a child. Try to be the best of parenthood and all that it should stand for. Take seriously the responsibilities that are part of parenting. By cultivating knowledge and wisdom about being a mother or father, you come to know the right things to do. Your children benefit, and correspondingly, you benefit too. You receive the satisfactions that come with being fully immersed in your life's roles. Life continues to unfold in its ever-changing cycles, as the *I Ching* predicts, and your offspring mature to live fully, perhaps one day becoming parents themselves.

A sage may be a parent, a laborer, an executive, an artist, a professional. This is normal and appropriate. The sphere of activity is the world that you are in. All are honorable roles and activities for the sage to engage in. All are opportunities to actually be the potential sage you are.

The Neo-Confucians added another dimension to learning when they investigated principle through li. The sage seeks to understand all about the world by exploring the principles, the very essence behind things. Thus the understanding gained is never superficial. Deep and careful thought must always accompany learning. Learning without thinking is a waste of time; thinking without learning is dangerous (paraphrased from the *Analects* 2-15, in Legge 1971, 150).

Confucians through the ages have valued wisdom that is relevant to living. The understanding you attain when thinking about what you have learned is lasting and useful. When you make your learning your own, you find yourself naturally applying it, doing the right thing at the right time.

THE NOBLE PERSON

Nobility is a matter of behavior, not of birth: Nobility is action, what we do, not just who we are by bloodline. If we can act in loving, benevolent ways, setting aside petty, small-minded concerns, we bring out nobility in ourselves and others. We move toward the qualities of the sage when we truly, graciously extend warmth and kindness. By being calm and at ease within, the sage inspires others to feel comfortable and at ease within too, like a host who makes his guests feel completely at ease. The comfort of acceptance, the security of the sage's benevolence, are the proper conditions needed to heal and evolve.

True sages are calm and tranquil. Calm comes from looking for the positive in situations as well as in the character of other people. We can just as easily interpret a half cup of milk as half empty or half full. Perspective is a function of how we interpret. Confucius pointed out that nobler persons emphasize the positive qualities in others and help them be that. The lesser person only sees the negatives.

When we look for the positive in our friends and associates, we permit and even encourage their best qualities. This positive path is one of happiness and fulfillment for everyone. From an empirical standpoint, modern research supports the value a positive attitude has on one's health. Heart disease patients with positive outlooks handle stress better, live longer, recover from illness quicker, and actually tend to have less heart trouble in the future (Spangler, 1999). Our hearts and minds are one, in a very literal sense.

Confucius encouraged his students to be the fully evolved human beings that their deepest nature contained, not simply for personal development but also for the development of others. There is hope for the world no matter how hard, at times, life may seem, if we improve ourselves.

Living the Confucian Way

Seek higher goals
To which you aspire
Don't base your actions
On lower desires
True happiness
Is not found
In mere pleasure
Benevolence is
An invaluable treasure
—C. Alexander Simpkins

Confucianism follows the Tao of Humanity. You do not have to look beyond yourself to find the best self that may lie hidden and undiscovered. You can cultivate yourself by following the Confucian Way. Your mental abilities sharpen, your sensitivities expand as you attune to the deeper principle in all things. You can stay aligned with the Mean to keep you on track as did the sages of antiquity, to live in human-hearted benevolence, fulfilled in your relationships and all that you set yourself to do with your life.

Part III applies Confucianism to everyday living. We present the ideal situation, just as Confucius did. But when implementing this wisdom, you may need to modify it or incorporate only parts of it to make it work for you.

CHAPTER 11

Meditation: Change Begins Within

The Way of learning is none other than finding the lost mind.
—Mencius

Knowing what comes first is important. Things have their roots and branches. The root of all wisdom comes when we make our thoughts and feelings sincere. This primary starting point brings us back to our own minds. Meditation offers a pathway.

Confucians believe that the true path is through our daily routines and relationships. Meditation helps you center yourself so that you can clearly discern your experiences and bring out the best qualities. As you sensitize your perceptions, sharpen your mental processing, and develop your awareness, your entire personality transforms. By cultivating yourself, you walk the same path as the sages of antiquity. Cultivation of the self begins with cultivation of the mind, which flows into everyday life.

The meditations in this chapter can help you develop inner calm and mental abilities. With a clear, discerning mind you can make wise choices and carry them into action.

QUIET SITTING

There are no direct instructions for meditation in Confucius and Mencius even though it is referred to. The later Neo-Confucians, influenced by Buddhism and Taoism's practice of meditation, devised a Confucian form of meditation they called quiet sitting.

True to the thrust of Confucian ideals, quiet sitting should only be performed when you have nothing else you must do. Meditation never justifies turning away from your work, friends, or family. Chu Hsi wrote,

> It will not do to give all this up, shut the door, sit quietly, and when things happen, refrain from dealing with them, saying "Wait for me to sit quietly," and not respond. (Chan 1989, 263)

Instead, quiet sitting is a method to enhance the quality of what you *do* in life; it should not take you away from it. We all have moments when there are no pressing obligations. Perhaps the children are asleep or a project you have been working on is finished. You may have only a few minutes or you might have an entire afternoon. When you do have some time without demands, no matter how short, you will find quiet sitting can be very beneficial.

Quiet sitting offers an opportunity to collect yourself. You assemble your thoughts so that they do not chase after superfluous ideas. Thus, it is a mental practice uniquely suited to the Confucian Way. This form of meditation is not a cutting off of thoughts. Rather, it involves gathering your thoughts so that they do not run away or lead you into unrelated distractions.

Chang Tsai explained quiet sitting: "At every instant something is pre-served. In every instant something should be nourished" (Chan 1989, 262). Thus, in sitting quietly you can develop a stable, calm center. Your thoughts become clearer and less distracted. You enhance concentration so that when you want to do something or learn something, you can focus your attention better. You can even improve your memory. This practice is healthy, refresh-ing, and nourishing to the mind.

Gathering your thoughts is not always easy to do at first. One student complained to Chu Hsi,

Every day when I am at leisure, I practice quiet sitting a little bit to nourish my mind, but I feel ideas naturally arising in profusion. The more I want to be quiet, the more disquiet I become! (Chan 1989, 261)

Chu Hsi told his student to realize that minds are naturally active. The student was instructed not to try to stop his thinking altogether. This could lead to mental stagnation. The important thing was not to think recklessly. Wang Yang-ming gave similar advice to a student who was trying to quiet his mind: "How can thoughts be stopped? They can only be corrected" (Chan 1963B, 190).

The quiet sitting exercises that follow develop mental skills. Experiment with them as often as you can. Even a few minutes per day can be beneficial.

Quiet Sitting I

Find a few moments when you do not have responsibilities calling on you. Go to a quiet room in your home, a pleasant park, or any place where you feel comfortable. Sit down. There are no exact rules for how to sit. If you'd like to sit on the floor, do so, but know that you can be just as successful with this med-itation sitting in a comfortable chair. Experiment. Find what's right for you.

Close your eyes. Sit for several minutes. Let your body settle, your breathing become calm, and your thoughts quiet somewhat. Keep your thoughts centered on this quiet moment. Try to keep your thoughts free of unnecessary or varied ideas. If you find your thoughts straying, gently bring your awareness back to this quiet moment. When your time for sitting is finished, return to your daily activities. Can you retain the inner calm?

Directed Quiet Sitting

Quiet sitting is an opportunity for your thoughts to become more focused, not scattered in a million directions. Your attention is then free to be directed where you want it to go. You can develop this ability further by deliberately focusing on one topic. Unlike some of the yoga meditations that concentrate attention on only one thing, Confucians prefer to have a broader area of focus, for discipline with flexibility.

Pick a topic to think about, then begin your quiet sitting as in the previous exercise. When you feel that you are relatively calm, turn your attention to the topic you have chosen. Think about it carefully and do not think about anything else. If your mind starts to wander, bring your attention back to your topic. Try to keep your thoughts clear and directed toward the topic. If your attention keeps wandering, or you feel sluggish, stop and resume another time. Otherwise, continue until your allotted time has passed.

QUIET AND ACTIVITY ARE ONE

Cheng-Hao believed that "Nature is calm whether it is in a state of activity or a state of tranquillity" (Chan 1963B, 191). Our original nature can be tranquil even in the midst of activity. Once you have become comfortable with quiet sitting you can bring it into your everyday life, guiding your mind back to its calm center throughout the day.

Quiet Sitting in Activity

Take a moment during the day, in the midst of an activity, to stop and sit quietly. You might find it easiest in the beginning to try it at home when you are doing a simple household task. Interrupt the action, sit down for one or two minutes, and allow your thoughts to gather as you did in the first quiet sitting exercise. It may help to remember that experience. When the time is up, return to the activity you were doing. Can you approach the task with renewed calm and awareness? Once you feel comfortable with this exercise, try it with more complex activities.

PUTTING YOUR MIND IN ACTIVITY

Confucians advised putting your mind into whatever activity you are doing. Whether active or quiet, speaking or silent, your attention must be there. This meditation applies the focus you have developed in quiet sitting to actively living your life.

Active Meditation

Take a brief walk for five to fifteen minutes. Pay close attention to the activity. Keep your mind focused on the walking. Notice the surface of the ground as you step, the temperature of the air on your skin, and any other sensations you have. Look around as you walk. Notice what you see and hear along the way. Permit and follow *relevant* thoughts, perhaps reflections on being in nature or observations of a bird or tree. Keep your thinking centered only on this experience. Do not let your attention drift to unrelated thoughts. If you find yourself distracted, bring your attention back.

Later, you can try this exercise with other activities. Always work toward keeping your attention focused on what you are doing. Allow related thoughts and associations, but do not follow unrelated, irrelevant thoughts.

DEVELOPING YOUR INNER SENSIBILITIES

We are all capable of recognizing the standard within. The pathway to follow is shown by sensitive attunement. We all eat and drink, but few of us distinguish the flavors. You can enhance your perception with training, using meditation.

Enhanced perception will help you discern, choose, and recognize principles. The exercises that follow help to heighten your sensibilities and develop experiences more fully while at the same time discriminating subtle distinctions.

Tasting

We all eat, but how often do we truly taste? Choose a food you like. Prepare it carefully; pay close attention as you get it ready. If you need to cook it, notice the aroma, appearance, temperature, consistency. When it is ready, sit down to eat. Eat slowly. Chew thoroughly. Describe the flavor of the food. Is it bitter, sweet, sour, salty? Feel the texture, consistency, and temperature in your mouth. How do you like it? Take the time to enjoy the experience.

Try to extend this kind of awareness to your regular meals. Can you keep your attention on the different qualities of the foods?

Tasting II

Now that you have practiced tasting, you can enhance your sensitivity. Try either tea or gourmet coffee. Pick a good quality beverage. When you begin to prepare it, use bottled water. Heat the water just to boiling and steep the tea or brew the coffee. As you wait, smell the aroma, observe the color. Now sip, slowly. Let it sit in your mouth for a moment as you distinguish the tastes. Is it smooth, tangy, sweet, bitter, light or heavy, sharp or smooth? How else can you describe it? Clear your palate with an unflavored biscuit or cracker, then taste again. Compare the different tastes.

Clear Perceptions Through Careful Observation

Being clear in your perceptions involves being alert and being observant. This exercise trains the ability to observe and recall.

Enter a room, perhaps one where you have not recently been. Look around for about one minute and then leave. Try to recall anything you remember about the room: the objects, their placement, the decor, the atmosphere. Return and compare the actual experience to your remembered one. What did you remember? What did you leave out?

Sit down and close your eyes for a few minutes of quiet sitting. Try to become aware of your experience and let your thoughts settle. Once you feel focused, open your eyes and enter the room again. Observe carefully for a minute and then leave the room. Try to recall what you observed. How many things did you notice the second time? How detailed was your description? Bringing quiet, focused attention to the task can help you to be more perceptive.

Sense of Smell

This exercise can be shared. Have a friend collect several aromatic objects: foods, plants, etc. Close your eyes and let your friend present the object for you to smell. Do not touch it. Describe the aroma. Is it sweet, sharp, smooth? Discern distinctions. Try to identify it as well. Do this with several different fragrances.

Sounds

Listen to an instrumental piece of music that you like. Close your eyes and listen carefully. Stop the music and recall the sounds. Then resume the playing. Notice the different instruments, the rhythms, the pauses, the tempo. Pay close attention; focus entirely on the sound. Describe it to yourself. Then listen to a very different kind of music. Compare and contrast the two sounds.

Enhancing your perceptions leads to the path. Do not separate sensitivity from your activities in daily life. Actively engage in relationships and endeavors, and be fully aware in each moment, using your cultivated perception.

CHAPTER 12

Benevolence in Government and Leadership

Tzu Lu asked for a hint on the art of governing. The Master replied:
Take the lead and set the example of diligent toil. Asked for a further hint,
he said: Be patient and untiring.
—Lionel Giles, *The Sayings of Confucius*

Confucius, Mencius, and Hsün-tzu spent many years of their lives advising officials and awakening nobler sensibilities and feelings for benevolence and justice in their rulers. Some rulers did experiment with the ideas and found them helpful.

Confucian ideas on government can be applied to any role in society. Confucius never took on a major leadership role in his lifetime, but he had a profound influence on those who were leaders. You do not have to be a leader to play an honorable role and have a positive influence on your world.

Whenever you are part of a group, you can experiment with this time-honored Confucian wisdom.

SINCERITY IN LEADERSHIP

People in society should take their roles seriously. Confucius explained this to Duke Ching of Chi when he told the duke that a ruler should *be* a ruler, a minister should *be* a minister, a parent should *be* a parent, a son or daughter should *be* a son or daughter (*Analects* 12.11, in Legge 1971, 256). People work toward attaining certain positions in life. Sometimes success comes suddenly. Other times, even after anticipating for a long time the taking on of a new position, some may not feel ready to wholeheartedly embrace the role. The self-concept, the idea we have about who we are and what we are capable of doing, may lag behind. This halfhearted involvement can lead to difficulties.

We had a client who was the head of his own small business. He hired a dozen employees who all looked up to him. He complained in therapy that he often felt uneasy when his employees asked him what to do. He disclosed that as a youth he had been very rebellious. He realized, suddenly, "Now I'm the authority I used to rebel against!" We worked with him to help him wholeheartedly embrace his role, here and now. His early experiences gave him empathy about his employees' concerns. He grew to be able to accept and use the expertise he had gained through the years of maturing to confidently become the leader he truly could be.

Accept your life-role. Work through your reluctant feelings or self-doubts. We encourage you to experiment for yourself with this exercise.

Exercise in Wholehearted Involvement

Practice quiet sitting for a few minutes to gather your thoughts. Then think about a role you have in life. Do you take the role seriously? Is it important to you? Do you fulfill your duties wholeheartedly or are you reluctant?

Do you feel capable or inadequate to handle things? Look for the inner pattern. Think about the importance of sincerely fulfilling your roles in life. Remember that deep within, human nature is good and capable. Can you be sincere in trying to develop your inner resources? If you can, you will find yourself naturally growing into the role.

GOODNESS AS ROLE MODEL

Everyone has the potential to be a shining example to others by embodying virtue. When the leader is fully functioning, others in the relationship, organization, or family function more fully as well.

> *He who exercises government [or family responsibilities] by means of virtue [te] may be compared to the north polar star, which keeps its place and all the stars turn toward it. (Analects 2-1, in Smith 1991, 178)*

The wise individual does more than talk about the importance of virtue; the wise individual actually acts virtuously. These actions speak for themselves and naturally become a role model to those around them.

Te Leads the Way

When leaders are righteous and benevolent, people naturally want to follow their directions. When leaders have unkindness or deception in their hearts, people naturally want to rebel. In this sense te, virtue, carries with it intrinsic authority. Force is unnecessary to make people cooperate. People will cooperate with the virtuous.

In fact, Confucius believed that power by force was ineffective. Without the consent of the people, government could not maintain its authority. Even Hsün-tzu said that human beings are the center, the foundation of culture. The ruler who has developed jen in his or her own person will gain the support of the people. There should be no need to enforce laws by threat of punishment. Both Confucius and Mencius used this metaphor to show the close relationship between the ruler and the people:

> *If you showed a sincere desire to be good, your people would likewise be good. The virtue of the prince is like the wind; the virtue of the people like grass. It is the nature of grass to bend when the wind blows upon it. (Smith 1991, 178–179)*

The relationship between government and the governed is a reciprocal one (shu). When working together in a group, each person keeps in mind the other person's needs. Tasks flow smoothly.

Feedback can be helpful at every level. Just as leaders should act correctly, the people must try to help their leaders stay on track. This passage from the *Classic of Filial Piety* shows how everyone in a society works together for mutual benefit:

> *In serving his superior the man of honor makes every effort to be faithful when he is in office . . . He encourages his superior in his good inclinations and tries to keep him from doing wrong. (Ebrey 1993, 68)*

Leading with Virtue

Leaders should put their own interests aside for the good of the people they lead. Mencius said that in any nation, the people should come first; the spirit of the land and grain are second, and the ruler is of least importance (paraphrased from the *Mencius* 7B-14, Legge 1971, 483).

Confucians assume that people want to be treated well. Leaders who put the interests of their people first will flourish. People will be happy to be cooperative because deep down they know that everyone benefits.

Confucius was asked by Tzu-kung, "What three things are most important for government?"

Confucius answered, "Adequate food, adequate weapons, and adequate confidence of the people."

Tzu-kung then asked, "If you had to give up one, which would it be?"

Confucius answered, "Weapons!" Tzu-kung asked, "What if you had to give up two?"

Confucius's answer clearly illustrates the importance of the people's morale. He said, "Food! There have always been deaths, but no country can survive without the confidence of the people" (paraphrased from the *Analects* 12-7, Chan 1963A, 39).

Morale and trust that someone can do a good job is important. Whenever you are working with other people, you must earn their trust and faith in your abilities and intentions by truly being and doing your best. Problems that might come along can be solved because everyone is working together in harmony.

CLEAR COMMUNICATIONS

Confucius was asked what he would do first when he took his job as administrator in the state of Wei. Confucius answered that he would begin by correcting names (*Analects* 13-3, Legge 1971, 263). The questioner was puzzled. How could using correct language make a difference in governing the state? Clear communications, where what you say matches what you mean, can make the difference between success and failure. Language is a way to indicate what something is and what should be done. When you express yourself clearly, people know what is expected and will be able to play their part well, in harmony with you.

The problem is that we often do not pay attention to ourselves as we communicate. Confucius believed that we should pause to think before speaking. It is better to say less and know more than to say more and know less. Take care in communications, as in all aspects of living. Smooth and effective leadership depends on careful, thoughtful communications. People often live without awareness of what they are saying. They do not take the time needed to express their thoughts with precision. These problems can be corrected.

Observing Communications

Next time you are speaking to someone, pay attention to what you say and how you say it. Do not change anything at first. Simply observe and take note. Listen to what they say in response. Follow the conversation from start to finish, keeping your attention focused on it.

Later, when you have some time to yourself, sit quietly. Think back on your conversation. Did your words match the meaning of the ideas you wished to communicate? Did you express your ideas clearly and directly? Did the listener seem to understand the meaning you intended? Did you respond to what the other person said?

Clarifying Language

If you felt that you did not communicate effectively with the other, reflection may help. Sit quietly for a few minutes. After your thoughts have cleared, examine the true significance behind or within what you were trying to say. Try to put it into words. Visualize a conversation with the person and remain in touch with your sense of li as you express yourself.

Begin with a single statement. How closely does this statement fit your idea? Modify the words until you come closer. Have you expressed the more fundamental principle? Keep searching for the correct words until you find them.

Careful Communications

Bring clarity of thought to your next actual significant conversation. Use the thinking you did in the previous exercises to maintain awareness of your words as you speak and of the words of others as they speak. Be thoughtful and expressive. Listen carefully when the other person speaks. Try to understand the underlying principle of what they are trying to say.

By living ethically and treating others well, you find yourself accomplishing what matters to you. The source is within, expressed in sincere, thoughtful, competent action.

**Strolling in the Valley by the Stream. Ink on
paper laid down on brocaded silk, Hanging
Scroll, 1959. San Diego Museum of Art (Gift of
Ambassador and Mrs. Everett F. Drumright)**

CHAPTER 13

Culture, Music, and Art: The Sound of Harmony

Art is a human activity having for its purpose the transmission to others of the highest and best feelings to which men have risen.
—Tolstoy, *What Is Art*

Human culture can reveal the flowering of human activity. Much of our creativity and loving kindness is expressed through culture when given the chance. The arts can be one of the highest influences, enriching us by its influence. Art has the power to free the soul and elevate humanity.

Confucius experienced this influence firsthand when learning to play a musical instrument. When he was twenty-eight years old, Confucius studied with Siang, a famous musician, who taught him to play on his lute a traditional musical piece composed by Wang, one of the ancient sages.

Confucius immediately performed well, and his teacher was pleased. However, Confucius felt that he had not truly mastered the piece and asked for more time to practice. His teacher gave him five days. When the five days were up, Confucius was still dissatisfied. Siang granted him five more days. Confucius practiced even harder. Finally, on the last day, Confucius approached his teacher with great excitement. "I have found what I have been searching for! As I played, I felt as if I was looking directly into Wang's eyes and heard his clear voice!"

Confucius had been transformed. Siang could see that Confucius had discovered the essence of the piece and begged Confucius to take him as his student. From this time on, Confucius wove music into the fabric of his philosophy. In music's wisdom, he learned to hear wisdom's music.

Harmony

> *Music hath charms to soothe the savage breast, to soften*
> *rocks or bend a knotted oak.*
> *—William Congrieve*

Long ago, people viewed music as symbolic of cosmic harmony. The ancient Chinese believed the entire universe was in continual motion, always changing with the passage of time, moving together in harmony. The *I Ching* expressed the continual flow of yin and yang, as yin gradually transforms into yang and yang changes back to yin. Their world pulsed and moved with the harmony of these continual changes.

Early Western philosophers held a similar view of a moving, pulsing universe. Pythagoras, the famous Greek mathematician, theorized that music is a reflection of the sounds produced by the planets as they move through their orbits. Aristotle thought that each planet moves at a different speed in its orbit and gives a different sound. This theory was called the Harmony of the Spheres:

Starting from this argument, and from the observation that their speeds as mea-sured by their distances are in the same ratio as musical concordances, they assert that the sound given forth by circular movement of the stars is a harmony. (Aristotle, in Deutsch 1984, 253)

Both East and West felt music was in their universe. Although modern science may not ascribe to these theories, you may have felt at times that you are in harmony with your environment. We can be in tune with the days, the night, when schedules synchronize well with the passing of time. We can be in tune with each season and its different cadence and timing. Take the time to find your rhythms between work, rest, and play. Be attuned to your world and the world around you.

Raising Your Emotions

Music can inspire our better emotions. Life is never bland or sterile when we listen to good music. As part of your inner cultivation, allow yourself to listen to some good classical music or other great music. Pick a composition that you find harmonious, inspiring, and uplifting. Allow yourself to become fully involved in listening. Do not distract your attention by doing something else at the same time. Feel your emotional reactions and enjoy the experience!

Cultured Experiencing

You can add culture to your life in simple ways, beginning with a very basic activity: sharing a meal. Invite some special people you care about to share a deliciously cooked meal with you. The food does not have to be expensive, but it should be carefully and delicately prepared. Set the table for-mally. Use your best dishes, silverware, napkins. Place everything in its exactly correct position. Have some soothing music playing softly in the background. Use candles or incense if you find these pleasing to your senses. When your guests arrive, treat them politely and respectfully. Sit down together and enjoy the meal. Savor the taste of the food and the quality of the conversation. Meditate respectfully on the relationship you share.

PAINTING

Chinese painting cannot be separated from philosophy. Just as Confucius viewed music as a way to help develop people, so painting also can have positive effects. In a book about painting called *Li Tai Ming Hua Chi*, written in 845, the author states,

> *Painting promotes culture and strengthens the principles of right conduct. It penetrates completely all the aspects of the universal spirit. It fathoms the subtle and the abstruse, serving thus the same purpose as the* Six Classics, *and it revolves with the four seasons. (Siren 1963, 7)*

Confucianism integrated with Taoism to become a guide in the approach and method of painting. The early *Six Canons* was a list of six standards for painters. This work was Taoist, inspired by the spirit of Tao as expressed through chi, the moving spiritual energy (see *Simple Taoism*).

Five hundred years later, two works were added to the *Six Canons*: the *Six Essentials* and the *Six Qualities*. These built on the Taoist roots but had strong Confucian orientations.

The First Essential was to reiterate the importance of the action of chi to help bring about powerful brushwork. The Second Essential introduced the Confucian idea that basic design should be according to tradition. Depth, beauty, and truth can be found in the past. Painters could draw upon this wonderful storehouse to inspire their work. The Third Essential stated that even though artists should express their originality, they must not disregard li, the principle or essence of the things they are painting. The Fourth Essential encouraged using color as it enriches the painting, and the Fifth Essential described spontaneity in handling the brush. The Sixth Essential developed the Confucian idea that painters should learn from the masters but avoid their faults. Confucius was careful to tell his students to be selective about who and what they follow. Pick out the good traits and avoid the bad ones.

Contemporary painters can be inspired in their own work by learning from tradition and the old masters. When an artist integrates the importance of li, principle, he explores his subject more deeply. Li uncovers the profound essence and reveals it in the work. This attention to li has given Chinese paintings a depth and life that keeps these ancient paintings vibrant for all who view them.

Painters can find a balance between personal original expression and staying true to the essence of the subject matter. Many paintings influenced by Confucian philosophy may not be exact representations; instead, the deeper nature of the landscape, the flower, the bird, is captured so perfectly that we almost feel as if we could take a walk through the mountains or hear the bird sing.

Attitudes for the Artist

Whatever you do in life, you can learn to approach your work correctly. Everything, whether large or small, should be handled with the same quality of order and attention.

A Chinese man named Kuo Hsi (1020–1090) learned this lesson by watching his father paint. Whenever his father was going to paint, he first carefully washed his hands. Next, he washed his inkstone and set out his inks and brushes. He placed incense on his left and put his materials to his right on a clean table near a bright window. As he performed this ritual, he showed respect for his materials and the process. He sat down and quietly gathered his thoughts. Only then did he begin to work.

Preparing to Work

The Confucian manner of approaching what you do begins with an orderly preset ritual. Always prepare your paints, brushes, and paper a certain way. Place them exactly on the table in the same place each time, whatever that is for you. Then sit quietly and allow your thoughts to gather around the subject you are planning to paint. Clear your mind of all unrelated thoughts.

Studying the Subject

Painters need to study their subjects carefully. For example, if you want to learn how to paint bamboo, bring a stalk out into the clear moonlight and place it so that its shadow falls on a white wall. In this way you will be able to study the li of its shape without distracting details like color, pattern, etc. You can apply this concept to anything you paint. For example, if you are working on a landscape, stand back and take in the entire scene. Notice the contours and shapes without attending to the details at first. Later you can study each detail, thoughtfully considering every aspect.

Painting with Jen

Once your mind is correctly set toward your subject, pay attention to the emotion you feel for your subject. Let your heart reach out, caring and open to your subject. Then, simply allow yourself to paint. As Mencius said, once your mind is filled with jen, you will naturally find yourself doing the correct thing.

Art Appreciation

Understanding Confucian philosophy can help you get more out of Chinese paintings. Chinese paintings were categorized by subject matter just as ceremonial rites and individual conduct was organized in an attempt to create harmony and order. Several systems of classifications were used, but the one that has been the most lasting gives four main categories: Landscapes (*Shan Shui*), People and Things (*Jen Wu*), Birds and Flowers (*Ling Mao Hua*

Hui), and Grasses and Insects (*Ts'ao Ch'ung*). These categories could be very exacting, but they were never intended to be rigid. Confucians placed their organization in relation to the continual change and fluidity expressed in the *I Ching,* and thus maintained fluidity in structure.

Chinese paintings have included subtle symbolism to uplift the viewer with an experience. Confucians believed art could ennoble us, and so painters often deliberately tried to awaken this in their viewers.

Primary symbolism, often expressed with circles and disks within the work, represented totality and harmony. Secondary symbols could be more subtle. Brushstrokes, color, or subjects such as the representation of a season or a pastoral scene could illustrate li. Interplay of yin and yang, dark and light colors, hard and soft textures were used carefully to express the deeper harmony that is always there.

In many of the paintings, though the subject is clearly recognizable, there is always a quality of the artist's individuality reaching out to express the true essence in the subject. This adds further depth and meaning to these works.

How to Look at a Painting

With these philosophical concepts in mind, you can gain a deeper appreciation for Chinese paintings. You must open yourself to the experience as Kuo Hsi said in his famous book, *The Great Message of Forests and Streams,* about viewing landscape paintings.

> *If one looks at them [landscape paintings] with a heart of the woods and the streams, their value becomes great, but if one looks at them with proud and haughty eyes, their value becomes quite low. (Siren 1963, 43)*

Being sincerely open to what the painting has to offer allows the viewer to experience the uplifting, ennobling effect that art can have. Do not close your mind to the potentials that are given.

Try to visit an art museum as part of your self-cultivation. Allow yourself to experience classic art, both Western and Eastern. Look for the deeper principle that is expressed. Feel the transmission of the artist's intent and let your emotions be refined by the experience.

Immerse yourself in cultural experiences on a regular basis, both at home in small ways and by sharing in the culture offered by society. Your spirit refines, adding depth and dimension to your character, as you walk the path to sagehood.

CHAPTER 14

Martial Arts: Honoring the Form

*Dig within. There lies the wellsprings of good: Ever dig
and it will ever flow.*
—Marcus Aurelius

Martial arts and Confucian philosophy are linked, though exactly how is sometimes obscured behind the tapestry of time's passing. Classical martial arts draw water from the well of Confucianism in many ways. The outlines and structures of the art itself, traditions of guidance, and primary qualities that form the character of the highly evolved martial artist can be traced to application of Confucian wisdom, whether deliberate or instinctive. Clear understanding of these links can enhance your potential for learning.

EARLY THREADS

During the Silla period in Korean history (A.D. 688–935), the three kingdoms on the Korean peninsula that had been at war with each other united under the Silla dynasty. Some attribute the victory of Silla to an indomitable martial arts force known as the Hwa Rang Do. Made up of youth from the noble classes, the Hwa Rang Do was a group dedicated to a moral code that trained their minds and spirits along with their bodies. Their code of conduct, inspired by Confucianism and Buddhism, included loyalty to the king, faithfulness to comrades, devotion to parents, bravery in battle, and a prohibition against senseless killing. By living and training according to this code, the Hwa Rang Do became a strong moral and military force for Silla. Confucianism was also one of the basic influences in Korean society, leading to Korean counterparts in formalities and codes of conduct in relationships.

Another group of early martial arts warriors were the samurai of Japan. These warriors, also known as Bushi, lived and died by what became known as the feudal code of Bushido, the military-knight Way. Bushido took centuries to develop, and like the European knight's code of chivalry, which was based on Christianity, the Bushido code derived from the ethical and spiritual values of religions Japan embraced: Zen, Shintoism, and Confucianism. Zen offered the samurai a method of meditation that allowed them to reach beyond words to a higher consciousness. The highest attainment for a master of Bushido was to be a master of Zen. Shintoism, the native religion of Japan, included reverence to ancestors and the spiritual quality of nature. Early Korea had a similar kind of indigenous nature worship of its own, including a variation of shamanism. Confucianism recognized this, and added a practical source of guidance, since knowledge was considered identical with its practical application: "To know and to act are one and the same" (Wang, in Nitobe 1969, 18). Ethical codes of conduct followed naturally from Confucian doctrine in terms of relationships between the samurai and his king, his father, his wife, and his friends.

In order to understand traditional martial arts, we must consider their original expressions in the feudal system of the past. The feudal system was an early attempt to guide conduct in such a way as to inspire and enhance the development of humanity. The knights of feudal times found higher values useful in their lives, helping them to be more effective. Through the power of inner truth, linking spirit with deeds in action, the threat to spirituality from unspiritual, destructive forces might be overcome. The threat of death could be faced with courage and honor.

The duty to uphold the lord and all that he symbolized became the honorable quest of the knights of Asia, as it did the knights of Europe. Warriors were organized around commitments, promises, and loyalty. If these vows were broken, dishonored, or corrupted, their efforts diminished and lost focused momentum. Death, preferable to dishonor, was often the result, whether by loss in battle or when commanded by the lord.

The purposeful Way of the warrior was founded on integrity. Integrity led to inner unity, and consequent inner strength. Inner strength was expressed in outer strength, manifested in action. The noble vow joined the warrior with the Way, committed to action. Dualities were resolved. The noble battle was a function of being true to inner truth.

SINCERITY

Sincerity was one of the highest virtues of the warrior-knights of the past as it is to the martial artist of today. When demands of life are met sincerely, all becomes possible. The way to be sincere in thought and action is through doing things wholeheartedly, unified, not halfway. It also leads to great power and focus in martial arts technique. Sincerity leads to wholehearted devotion and involvement.

HONOR AND RESPECT

Derived from original threads, the feudal system has today become interwoven into the fabric of traditional martial arts, though in modified form. We do not have lords or princes, but we do have role hierarchies within our culture. Modern martial art is more than just a set of techniques and skills. It is an art, a *Way* that "Does not limit itself to proficiency in technique as an end in itself but goes further, to integrate the art as a way of being in the world" (Chun 1976, 11).

According to the famous Japanese martial artist Mas Oyama, martial arts begin and end in courtesy. Respect, honor, and integrity are primary virtues in martial artists as they are in Confucianism.

Traditional martial arts emphasize respect and loyalty for the *sensei*, the instructor, as well as the system itself. Traditional arts have a hierarchy of instructors up to masters, then to grandmaster. Honoring the teacher is the counterpart of filial piety. The teacher, the sensei, is highly respected by the students, and in turn, the sensei honors the student with respectful, correct, and careful teaching. Students should never disrespect the teacher. Their task, throughout the teaching relationship, is to sincerely try to carry out what the sensei requires. Attitude matters in learning. The student bows to the tradition, and this forms character, enabling martial arts teachers to communicate correct patterns of movement, and students to express the style's spirit. Sincere and open receptivity of the student makes this possible.

The sensei, in turn, is respectful of the students, and is expected to take his role of teacher seriously and sincerely. This attitude assists in the learning process. Teachers teach and students learn, and all find themselves doing better and getting along in a special brotherhood. This special relationship becomes a trust between them. If maintained, both are raised up, to become wiser and better than they were before the interaction. Within this structure are opportunities to fully be and to express virtue in action, the Confucian Way.

In traditional schools, students who strive and dedicate themselves to the art are recognized and rewarded according to the personal efforts made. Students receive in reciprocal relationship to what they give. They progress and are granted a progressively more honored place in the hierarchy of the system, according to loyalty, years spent learning, level of commitment, and personal skill. The classical spirit of the style is perpetuated in its correct form through the enthusiastic participation of its members. The Confucian ideal of finding the best in antiquity is passed along by practicing these traditional martial arts systems.

THE SENSE OF JUSTICE

Martial artists evolve their own sense of justice. Though they develop power from training, they learn to use it wisely. Training imbues practitioners with the spirit of steadfastness in the relentless day in and day out of steady disciplined practice. True enlightenment comes through practice—that is, *doing* is meditation. It is in the act itself that ethical value comes to life. Confucius believed that virtue must always be expressed in action, by what people do in everyday life. Mencius added that benevolence is the mind and justice the path. He beseeched people to follow this path, recognizing its importance: "How lamentable is it to neglect the path and not pursue it, to lose the mind and not know to seek it again!" (Nitobe 1969, 67).

Today's traditional martial arts incorporate this sense of justice in the ethical codes that students adopt: to use their martial art for defense only, never as the initiator of an attack. As a concrete manifestation of this principle, forms begin with a block, not an attack. Traditional training teaches through action.

Spiritually evolved martial artists do everything they can to avoid petty fighting. By developing a strong character through their training, they are not easily drawn into fights. The principle of defense is to prevent harm to themselves and, therefore, others, thereby preserving and remaining part of the harmony. This strong sense of justice is a guiding principle for the martial artist in action. Tae kwon do grandmaster Son Duk Sung speaks for all martial artists who follow the higher path when he said:

As the skill develops, the inner sense of responsibility develops along with it, making the person skilled in Tae Kwon Do a better member of the community than he was before. Having the power to kill, he is less likely to use any power or force at all than he was before. (Son and Clark 1968, 18)

HUMILITY

Confucians teach, similar to Buddhists, that the humble person is the truly wise one. Confucius said that the strong, the enduring, the simple, and the modest are closest to virtue.

A person who acquires great strength and capacities from martial arts training might be expected to become arrogant. The virtue of humility, central to martial arts training, keeps the personality in balance. Receiving and accepting correction requires humility, which is sometimes defined as the absence of pride. For every yin there must be yang; humility and pride are opposite poles of the same thing. Accomplished martial artists also have confidence in their skills, and these skills can be applied to other aspects of life. Knowing this, they feel it unnecessary to continually prove themselves. The truly great martial artist will appear humble in deference to higher values.

FORMS: LI IN MOTION

Forms are patterns of movements, passed along from generation to generation—the classic literature of martial art. Like performing a Confucian ritual, practicing forms with intensity and sincerity communicates the spirit of the art and offers the student a standard for perfection.

The movements included may be specific to the style of the founder or they may be a variation of fundamental root forms whose origins are obscure but are now part of the repertoire of traditional martial arts. Forms are used selectively in certain styles for shaping, molding, and training students in the style's rhythms and techniques. And through them students gain control, precision, and timing, along with a resource for deeper understanding and creative inspiration.

Students can study and analyze their forms for useful meanings as they repeat them over and over. These forms are then used to evaluate the student's control, abilities, understanding, and progress. Proper evaluation, of course, requires a criterion or standard against which to gauge the student's progress.

Classical forms help with this, since there is a certain way to perform each one, an exact positioning and a definite spirit. Certain forms are appropriate for each level of the student's progression, and can be used by a skilled sensei to determine whether the student is entitled to advance or else exhibits defects that prevent progress.

When students start to learn to perform a form well, it is because they have begun to realize the deeper understandings that are implied in the multilevel meanings and patterns. Learning arises directly from the principles encoded in the movements.

PERFECTING THE SELF THROUGH LIFETIME LEARNING

Martial arts should be studied with the goal in mind of perfection: perfection of form in movement, perfection of mind in activity, perfection of the li within the system. Therefore, to achieve true mastery, you must not move from one school to another, hoping to learn more varied techniques. Learn the art to its roots. Strengthen and extend the roots; the many branches follow naturally. The higher goal of mastery is more important than just accumulation of disharmonious techniques.

With wisdom comes the recognition that there is always more to learn. Learning is infinite, ceaseless throughout life. Learning in martial arts is a stepwise process. As the student progresses in ability a new belt is awarded, until the student reaches Black Belt. With each elevation of rank comes additional responsibility and role expectations, not just recognition and reward. The black belt is more than just an award. It is a part of the martial artist's identity, an attitude for approaching life's challenges with strength, courage, discipline, and respect. There is a deeper understanding among accomplished practitioners that earning a black belt is not the end but only the beginning. The way to the source of virtue lies within each person. Train hard, then you will find wisdom's Way.

CHAPTER 15

The Path to Wisdom

The price of wisdom is above rubies.
—The Old Testament

Learning is a highly valued activity for the Confucian sage, the path to enlightenment. Continuing to learn, we engage in the quest for greater wisdom, always pointing toward improvement in action.

The world around us can be studied for the timeless patterns of principle that are expressed in everything and everyone. We can meditate on our relationships with others and learn, for learning links us to our true nature, an inseparable part of the world of people, objects, and events. Understanding this requires effort, a serious commitment to extract the pearl from the oyster of everyday experience. The person who learns but does not think is lost.

Find the Wisdom

As you journey on the path of your daily life, observe carefully. Watch events and consider the ultimate significance of your own life's circumstances.

Life as you live it is the ground in which true, classical wisdom can be found. Think of some meaningful experience that you have had. Take a few moments to sit quietly and be with that experience. What do you think and feel about it? What can you learn from it? What individual essence of Confucianism's true wisdom do you discern in this experience? How does it apply to your life?

LEARNING AND ACTION ARE ONE

Learning leads to thought, thought leads to knowledge, knowledge leads to action and around again in a continuous circle, with no separation or stopping. The function of learning and knowing is its expression in action, in relationships as well as all human endeavors. Engage in a correct, honorable, and continuous flow of action in the world.

Most people know what they should do, but often cannot make themselves do it. Forcing yourself to do something, even if you know it is for your own good, is not effective. Engage your mind first, deeply and sincerely, then action will flow naturally. For example, research shows that people who have a problem with alcohol can be helped by learning about the condition. So all alcohol and drug rehabilitation programs include some teaching. Education about the dangers, the negative effects on the body, the progression from years of use, along with learning how to cope better with emotions and relationships, help people change.

If you have been trying to accomplish something but have been unable to take action, experiment with the Way. Immerse yourself in the topic. Read about it, talk to people who are knowledgeable, gather as much relevant information as you can. Do not bother with unimportant details. Look for the li, the underlying principles. Fill your consciousness with it. If you sincerely involve yourself in the topic, action will naturally follow. Start with correct knowledge to perform correct action.

DEVELOPING WISDOM

Wisdom is the outcome from remaining true to principle within the interpersonal realm as well as in the realm of objects. Confucianism does not point us away from the everyday world, it directs our focused attention to this world. In turn, this enables us to evoke and develop greater understanding of the essence of truth that is symbolically present in the objects and circumstances of this world. This leads to wisdom. But Confucian wisdom is not transcendental, not a transformation of the world itself, which is actually real though in a process of transformation. Wisdom is immanent in the actual situations of everyday life, available for everyone who sincerely seeks to know.

Knowledge should be extended in every way, not merely academically or through one's job. Anything can be used to begin, a window that opens to show us greater understanding, a vision of wisdom. Disciplined sincere investigation can lead to action. Action with thought can lead to deeper knowledge. Yet wisdom and knowledge are not always linked. Wise individuals are not always learned ones, and learned ones are not always wise. The ideal is to bring them together, as one, in thought and action. We learn by doing. We do things in order to learn.

DRAWING FROM THE PAST: HONOR AND RESPECT

By researching the classical traditions and customs of the past, Confucius found valuable lessons for human relationships and nature. Exemplary kings of the past lived honorably, showing respect. Goodness was rewarded while evil bore its inevitable fruits, often resulting in punishment. These lessons taught about the patterns of flowing change as well as insight into the stable constancies of life. The past, considered as multifaceted, is a resource to learn from and use. But this does not necessarily take place automatically, as a matter of course. We all know people who have experiences but do not learn from them. One day, they learn and their experience is forever changed.

Learning can take place now. Confucianism encourages you to experience, to learn, and to think about it.

Confucius lived in feudal times, which led to his use of feudal relationships to exemplify virtue, but the principle behind these examples can also be applied to modern times and modern relationships, with appropriate correction and changes in roles. We live in more enlightened times with regards to norms of life roles, class, gender, race, and creed, but we have a long way to go. We need more than ever to practice love, respect, benevolence, and honor with each other. The world is always changing, yet the true forms and patterns within remain.

True form, from examples of better moments of ideal functioning in the past, glows within wise people, important events, and great potential. Through study and deep contemplation, purified essences of the best qualities may be distilled, crystals assembled. Templates emerge to use, to mold, and to shape the future from the uncarved block of potential. Honor and sincere respect naturally follow the virtue of ideal forms in the better moments of the past. The ideal becomes real by active striving in the present to transform the future.

HUMANITY IS YOUR TEACHER

We can learn from all the people we encounter from all walks of life, with different levels of knowledge. We need only pay sincere attention and realize the deeper implications in order to learn from them. Dogen, founder of the Soto Zen sect, learned from a thoughtful conversation with a humble cook the deep wisdom that changed his life and helped him guide his sect. Everyone has something to teach us if we take the time to listen.

Learning From Others

Think of a real person in your life, someone who is an ideal source of inspiration for you, someone with qualities you want or need to learn. This person may be a parent, a good friend, a teacher/role model, a civic leader, a great artist, or a professional you deeply respect. Seek the higher form within the everyday form, the ideal expressed in what they actually thought or did.

Begin by respecting what you hear when they say something you consider wise and commendable or when they do something you believe exemplifies correct conduct. Try to penetrate its wisdom, the personal meaning it has for you. Then write it down in a journal to yourself.

Good character and integrity do not just happen of themselves. These qualities develop from your own efforts. Good character and integrity are the natural expression of innate goodness, true human nature.

Learning From Exemplary People

Think about someone you find inspirational—this can be a famous person or someone in your neighborhood. Learn about his or her life as if a biography has been written, or listen to the person's life story. Think about how this individual overcame personal struggles and setbacks. Consider what is exemplified, the lessons that were learned. For example, if your goal is to become a statesman, study an eminent leader like Winston Churchill or George Washington. How did they do it? Let yourself learn from them as you would learn from a great teacher. But recognize that you can learn from anyone, not just famous people, if you search the depths within the human heart.

SEEK THE SAGE

Like the perfume of an exotic flower, wisdom permeates everyone. Many years ago, we stood in line at a ticket booth in Grand Central Station, calmly waiting our turn. People pushed impatiently forward, carrying suitcases, harried and aggravated by the long wait. Some cursed, yelled, and shoved. By the time we got to the front of the line, we felt impatient ourselves. But we were greeted by a breath of springtime. The ticket agent smiled and in a calm, soothing voice said, "How may I help you?" We were so overcome by his tranquillity that we asked him how he managed to stay so calm amid such chaos. With a gentle smile he answered, "One at a time," and then competently took care of our tickets.

As you go through your day, whenever you talk to someone or listen to a conversation, look for a gem of classical wisdom being expressed, for the sage behind the person. You will be surprised how often the sage appears! Note it down when you observe the spirit, and keep it for future meditation.

DO NOT DO WHAT YOU SHOULD NOT DO

To know what you do not know is wisdom in knowledge. Similarly, not to do what you should not do is wisdom in action. Awareness of boundaries and restraint, inhibition of the wrong, can help you find the correct path. Form is not doing in another way. With a simple exercise Mencius instructed people in practicing "not doing" to help them find their correct path.

When you say to yourself, "I would never do that," apply that same strength of conviction to something you want to do but cannot quite find the motivation to accomplish. For example, most people feel strongly that they would never deliberately be mean. You can use this conviction when you lose your temper to keep yourself from saying and doing things you might regret later. Mencius believed that we all have inner strength within us. The trick is to appropriately apply these abilities for our benefit.

LEARNING TO TEACH; TEACHING TO LEARN

Teaching and learning are inseparably linked. Confucius noted that teaching exposes a teacher's weaknesses and shortcomings and motivates the teacher to learn, not just the student. Responding to the student is stimulating to the teacher. Teaching completes the cycle of learning. Teaching is the other pole of the yin-yang, as learning requires being receptive, teaching requires being active. The teacher guides the student to comprehend the principles of the subject, contributing with meaningful presentations. Teachers should guide and gently encourage their students, not attempt to push them into learning; if they do, students will lose interest and dislike learning for themselves. They will do the minimum and turn away from its fulfillment in wisdom.

Learning Skills: Reading

Reading can be a great source for learning on your own. Begin by sitting quietly for a few minutes. Bring your attention to the activity that you are about to begin. As you read a passage, read at a speed that allows you to comprehend. If you find that you are not understanding, slow down. Engage your thoughts around the subject matter. If you have ideas, stop for a moment to think about them. Then return to the reading. Do not push yourself to read more than you can read with understanding. If you only read one paragraph and sincerely think about it, you have read successfully.

Learning Attitudes

The rationalist Neo-Confucians suggest that we approach learning in a particular way. They believed that the mind is the ruler and analytical reasoning is the way to learn and acquire knowledge, setting the sincere student on the path.

Chu Hsi encouraged his students to study diligently, get in touch, and then follow the li of the subject they were learning. Act according to the spirit and the Way of the ancients. Respect what you see and put into practice what you know. Be honest, sincere, and tranquil in learning. Take each task seriously, whether large or small, complex or simple. The principle is inherent in the individual Tao. Principle is in all things, expressed in individual principles. Search for li with all your heart.

Learning can take place whatever your circumstances, whether wealthy, comfortable in moderation, or poor. Live and work accordingly. Tao is true to what is. Regard all circumstances equally.

While we learn, we learn *how* to learn, the class or context of learning. This is implicit in Confucian thought. We learn how to learn and can thereby learn other things of a similar nature. For example, the first foreign language can be very difficult to master. But the second new language is a little easier, and by the third or fourth language, people find the learning much more rapid. This is because they have learned *how* to learn languages. Principles have far more usefulness than mere memorization or rote learning, which is bound to the single context.

LEARNING HOW TO LEARN BY FINDING LI

When learning, try to extract the deeper organizing principle behind or within the matter, not just the details. Search for the ruling pattern, the guiding principle that distinguishes it. For example, American woodworkers are very familiar with the dovetail saw. It is used to cut fine joinery and cuts on the push stroke. The teeth of the saw are slightly angled to make the saw cut cleanly on the push stroke. Japanese woodworkers use a dozuki saw. This saw is used for the same purpose—to cut fine joinery—but it cuts on the pull stroke. Here the individual principle of each type of saw is different, yet the universal principle of sawing is the same. The principle of sawing is general, the particular principle of each type of saw is specific. Principle precedes function. When you understand the underlying principle, the function becomes clear.

Finding Li

Look for the underlying li in things. If you are trying to learn something, look for the principles. The detailed data then becomes easier to remember. Distinguish between the specific li and the more general li, as in the differences between dozuki and back saws versus sawing in general. Once you can become aware of the li, you will be able to apply it in useful ways.

CHAPTER 16

From Cultivation to Actualization

Confucius said, Perhaps others can do it the first time; I must do it ten times; perhaps others can do it the tenth time; I must do it a thousand times. But he who really has the perseverance to go this way—be he foolish, he will become clearheaded; be he weak, he will become strong.
—Karl Jaspers, *Socrates, Buddha, Confucius, Jesus*

SELF-ACTUALIZATION: BECOMING YOUR BEST

Look within to find the source of change. We evolve to higher levels by becoming more deeply ourselves. Be in harmony with the universe from the center. Falseness, sham, and hypocrisy lead us away from the center, thereby affecting our ability to function well. Sincerity and honesty with ourselves lead us back to the center. Cultivation of the inner self leads to development of great potential in outer endeavors.

Aim for the highest, most perfect goodness within. Then your life is perfectly centered, turning on the axis of the human heart in respectful relationship to others. We are all human; our actions should inevitably be guided by human-heartedness, our jen.

Self-cultivation leads to self-actualization. Knowledge and thought leads to actions of the higher self. Being true to form, to li, leads to fulfillment of the highest potentials. Higher principles lead naturally to personal integrity. Correct being, authenticity, leads to higher functioning: the farther reaches of human nature. Thus, following the inner order brings harmony to social situations, better leadership, better families, and a better world.

Human nature is unique. Theories of human nature and interaction that would reduce human beings to the level of animals are not acceptable to the Confucian point of view. People seek value, meaning, and purpose in life. Merely trying to reduce tension is not enough of a motivation for action, nor is it the essence of health and happiness. Just reducing tension is negative, a lower level of functioning. Often we pursue challenges that may lead to stress and tension; higher education, a challenging and demanding job, climbing a mountain are a few examples. Life without meaning or purpose is empty and intolerable. Human beings must engage in purposeful personal striving. Seek happiness by setting out on a journey to the highest goals imaginable. We are born with a sense of direction. The compass is the human heart.

The same goal is shared by this Catholic monk:

> *Spiritually elevate yourself, at least once a day, at a predetermined time, to contemplate and long for your own goal, in its broadest understanding and reaches, and in its highest perfection. (Caputo 1997, 53)*

PERFECTION IS HERE AND NOW
In Soto Zen Buddhism, all things interpenetrate with no separation: *satori*. Every breath, every movement, every action taken is an opportunity to

practice meditation, and practice is enlightenment. No separation is possible; everything is part of the whole, of the Oneness of the universe. The significance of each part is a function of its participation in the whole. Similarly, in Confucianism, every action taken, including every moment of every human relationship in which you participate, is an opportunity to follow the Tao of humanity, to help create a shared positive world through practicing jen. No separation is possible. By living sincerely, in accord with the primary virtues, better living happens. Perfection can be possible here and now in your everyday interactions when you follow and are true to the perfection already present within you.

LIVING LIFE'S ROLES FULLY

Your natural talents, expressed in the roles given you and your vocation, are your individual destiny, to meet and work out. Every word you speak, every experience you have should be taken seriously. Each experience, each moment of relating is an opportunity for deep learning.

You are inescapably in relationship with the significant others in your life: your parents, your brothers and sisters, your friends. Everything you do, everything you say is related to others as well as yourself. You are in unity with the significant relationships of your life. All your interpersonal interactions give you an opportunity to show love, honor, and respect toward your family, your friends, and your fellow human beings. Every action you take in the world is a step toward this, in a positive direction, or a step away from this, in a negative direction.

Sincere day-to-day living is the context for expressing yourself. You make virtue advance through your own true, sincere actions, or recede if you are untrue to the genuine, true goodness within you. Dishonor and disharmony follow insincerity. This standard is not subject to social or pragmatic expediency, but answers to the higher calling within. Interpersonal situations are not so simple and straightforward that we should judge them superficially. Honor and respect for loved ones requires tolerance, granting them flexibility in social interactions.

Reflection on Wholehearted Sincerity

Sit quietly when you have some free time. Let your thoughts gather in the quiet moment. Once you feel relatively calm, think about your life's roles: your work, your family, your friends. Ask yourself if you have been sincere in your endeavors. Do you put forth your best effort or not? Is your attention easily distracted? Do you give less than your best? Reflect on these things with this emphasis: Sincerity comes first. Let your thoughts stay with this topic until you have explored it fully.

LIVING WITH JEN: BENEVOLENCE, KINDNESS, HUMAN-HEARTEDNESS

Correctly performing your responsibilities to others is part of performing your duty to yourself. Since we are in relationship as an inseparable part of our humanity, we cannot disregard this in order to fulfill ourselves. But we also cannot disregard fulfilling ourselves personally either, as an inseparable part of our duty to humanity. This paradox is resolved in living with jen.

These qualities come from within. All human beings share a common human nature. Consequently, human beings have innate knowledge that can help in distinguishing between right and wrong. Difficulties arise when people turn away from their built-in capacity. Focus on your inner voice for virtue.

You can begin to bring jen into your life by focusing your thoughts on it. Then your actions will be guided by these classical virtues, naturally and calmly. Consider how you might act in accord with your intuitions of benevolence. You might think about specific situations with people you care about. As Confucius himself admitted, being consistently virtuous was a challenge to work toward, even for him.

IMPROVING YOUR INTERPERSONAL RELATIONSHIPS

Confucius defined certain relationships as central, including parent to child, sibling to sibling, friend to friend. Filial piety is the central axis of primary relationships, where "filial" involves duty, respect, and affection. These qualities can nourish a relationship, enhancing the bond. Certain obligations always accompany any relationship, but if both people perform their part sincerely, the interaction transforms both, evoking their best qualities. Both participants will evolve, to grow together as persons.

Exercise to Improve Relationships

Begin with a few minutes of quiet sitting to gather your thoughts. Focus your attention on a significant role you play in your life: parent, son or daughter, friend, employer or employee, government official or citizen. Think about higher ideals for this role. What is the highest potential for being a good parent, a diligent son or daughter, an effective and responsible boss, a productive worker, a caring helper, a good citizen? Think of exemplars from the past—people who embodied and expressed the best qualities of their role. How could you make these qualities your own? In what way could you fulfill the potential of your own roles? What would you need to do? How could you improve yourself? Begin with a small, achievable action—a symphony is composed one note at a time. Approach it with an open mind, with sincerity and caring for what you are trying to do and be.

Attention to Relationship

If you would like to improve a relationship in your life, begin by turning your mind to it. Next time you are with this person, sincerely pay attention to each point in the interaction. Keep your attention fully focused on the experience and the feelings you have. How do you act, moment to moment, with this person? Do you express your human-heartedness? Are you sincere, honestly present, and caring? Can you be respectful?

Applying the Silver Rule

Everyday situations in this world are an opportunity to live the silver rule, to treat others as we wish they would treat us. When we live with jen, with benevolence and kindness, we find inner fulfillment. Other people's actions do not have to force you to deviate from your Path. Instead, their behavior offers you an opportunity to reach out with human understanding. We often do not know the negative forces that bring others to the point of negative conduct. We have not lived their life. We can trust that deep within each human being there is a positive human nature lying dormant.

Living by the Silver Rule I

Sit quietly in meditation in order to gather your thoughts about a certain person in your life who seems to be behaving negatively toward you. Do you lack compassion? How has this person's personal life been difficult? What forces and experiences had a negative influence? Can you be honorable and respectful of the greater humanity of the other, not just react to the momentary transitory expression, their temporary relationship? Sometimes, when you can turn your attention toward universal symbols, particular individual situations can be moderated better.

Living by the Silver Rule II

Sit quietly and think carefully about the silver rule. Do you lose your direction when people do not treat you as you wish to be treated? Are you making your self-esteem contingent on their actions toward you? Remember, the silver rule frees you from having your self-esteem dependent on other people. You have the choice to act correctly and thereby feel good about yourself. Think about the potential. You will feel satisfaction, contentment, and happiness when you courageously do the right thing in spite of circumstance. Experiment with the silver rule in an everyday interaction. Notice how you feel.

SEARCH YOURSELF

Mencius was often asked how we can cope with people who treat us badly. He responded that you must look within. Observe your own feelings, thoughts, and behavior. What are you telling yourself about the other person? Are you saying to yourself that he or she should not do this to you and then feeling angry about your own thoughts? These thoughts and feelings may be adding to your feelings of discomfort with the person. Try to recognize the negative thing you are doing and *stop* doing it. Take into account the love or caring you also feel for this person. Correct yourself by being true to your center. Then you will be free to cope with the other more benevolently.

KEEP YOUR INTEGRITY

If you have tried every change possible and are truly and sincerely in accord with jen, but someone still seems to treat you poorly, recognize that the other person may not be in accord with jen, not functioning at his or her best. Without staying true to their center, like ignoring the compass, people may lose their way. This may not change for now. The superior person does the correct thing, which is in his or her own power to do. Do not fret and worry about what cannot be changed. Do not sacrifice your personal integrity. Remember, your benevolent action need not depend on reciprocation. Your guiding values flow from the absolute, from Tao. You are free to act correctly and benevolently.

ONENESS WITH TAO

Keep true to your inner spirit, the benevolence within. You can rely on your integrity to give you strength and courage when you live with love. You can understand what is happening in your world when you investigate the deeper principles. Return to your center to guide you and you will navigate smoothly, no matter how choppy the waters of life become.

CONCLUSION

According to Confucius, we must open our eyes, look, and see, or wisdom will shine only in shadow and not brighten our intellect with its light through the windows of our perception. From the darkness and shadow of ignorance come the errors and misconceptions that lead to the problems and evils of life.

We must open our ears, listen, and hear the voices and music of our primary relationships. They will speak to us of what is needed, how to act, and what to do. When we do not hear or respond, then we lose touch with Tao, and our world is thrown into chaos and misfortune.

Learning and knowledge take a lifetime of effort that can only be achieved with full, wholehearted attention and sincerity. We must take our lives seriously and strive toward the highest potential we can imagine. Difficult though it may be at times, day by day, we must live with human-heartedness. Then the light of wisdom will shine in our lives, and the music of our personal relationships will resonate with true harmony.

We act, and the fruits
Of our actions ripen
To be
Borne on winds of destiny
—C. Alexander Simpkins

THE THREE SOVEREIGNS
Legendary

Fu-hsi, the Ox-tamer
2852 B.C.

•

Shen-nung, the Divine Farmer
2737 B.C.

•

Huang-ti, the Yellow Emperor
2607 B.C.

THE THREE SAGE KINGS
Legendary

Yao
2356-2347 B.C.

•

Shun
2244-2205 B.C.

•

Hsia dynasty
2205-1751 B.C.
(beginning with Yü)

SHANG DYNASTY
1751-1112 B.C.

CHOU DYNASTY
1111-249 B.C.

Spring and Autumn Period
722-481 B.C.

•

Confucius
552-479 B.C.

•

Warring States Period of Chou
480-221 B.C.

•

Mencius
371-289 B.C.

•

Hsün-tzu
298-238 B.C.

CH'IN DYNASTY
221-207 B.C.

Burning of the Books
213 B.C.

•

Building of the Great Wall

HAN DYNASTY
206 B.C.- A.D. 220

Tung Chung-shu
179-104 B.C.

•

Wen-Ti
179-159 B.C.
Confucian emperor

•

Wu-ti
140-87 B.C.
Confucian emperor

Ch'in dynasty
265-420
Decline of Confucianism, rise of Taoism and Buddhism

South and North dynasties
420-589

Sui dynasty
581-618

T'ang Dynasty
618-907
Confucian revival

Five Dynasties
907-960

SUNG DYNASTY
960-1279
Neo-Confucians

Chou Tun-I
1017–1073

•

Chang Tsai
1020–1077

•

Cheng–Hao
1032–1085

•

Cheng–I
1033–1108

•

Hsiang–shan
1139–1193
Lu–Wang School of Mind

•

Chu Hsi
1130–1200
School of Principle

YUAN DYNASTY (MONGOL)
1271-1368

MING DYNASTY
1368-1644

Wang Yang-ming
1472-1529
Lu-Wang School of Mind

BIBLIOGRAPHY

Aurelius, Marcus. 1981. *Meditations*. New York: Penguin Books.

Blyth, R. H. 1964. *Zen and Zen Classics*. Vol. 1. Tokyo: Hokuseido Press.

Bruce, Percy J. 1922. *The Philosophy of Human Nature*. London: Probsthain & Co.

Caputo, Fr. Louis. 1997. *Ascension*. Newark, N.J.: Vocationist Fathers.

Chan, Wing-tsit. 1963A. *A Source Book in Chinese Philosophy*. Princeton, N.J.: Princeton University Press.

_____. 1989. *Chu Hsi, New Studies*. Honolulu: University of Hawaii Press.

_____. 1963B. *Instructions for Practical Living and Other Neo-Confucian Writings by Wang Yang-ming*. New York: Columbia University Press.

Chang, Chi-yun. 1957. *A Life of Confucius*. Taipei, Taiwan: China News Press.

Chun, Richard. 1976. *Tae Kwon Do: The Korean Martial Art*. New York: Harper and Row Publishers.

Creel, H. G. 1954. *Chinese Thought from Confucius to Mao Tse-tung*. London: Eyre & Spottiswoode.

Dawson, Raymond. 1981. *Confucius*. Oxford: Oxford University Press.

Deutsch, Diana. 1984. "Musical Space" in *Cognitive Process in the Perception of Art*. Edited by W. R. Crozier and A. J. Chapman. North Holland: Elsevier Science Publications B.V.

Dobson, W.A.C.H. 1969. *Mencius*. London: Oxford University Press.

Ebrey, Patricia Buckley, ed. 1993. *Chinese Civilization: A Sourcebook*. New York: The Free Press.

Elwes, R.H.M., trans. 1955. *Benedict de Spinoza*. New York: Dover Publications.

Emerson, Ralph Waldo. 1926. *Essays by Ralph Waldo Emerson*. New York: Thomas Y. Crowell Company.

Fisher, Mary Pat. 1994. *Living Religions*. Englewood Cliffs, N.J.: Prentice Hall.

Fung, Yu-lan. 1966. *A Short History of Chinese Philosophy*. New York: The Free Press.

Gernet, Jacques. 1972. *A History of Chinese Civilization*. Cambridge: Cambridge University Press.

Giles, Lionel. 1998. *The Sayings of Confucius*. Middlesex, England: Tiger Books International.

Huang, Kerson. 1984. *I Ching, The Oracle*. Singapore: World Scientific Publishing Co. Pte Ltd.

Jaspers, Karl. 1962. *Socrates, Buddha, Confucius, Jesus*. San Diego: Harvest/HBJ Book.

Legge, James. 1970. *The Works of Mencius*. New York: Dover Publications, Inc.
_____. 1971. *Confucius*. New York: Dover Publications, Inc.

Lester, Will. July 3, 1999. "Morality Crisis." New York: Associated Press.

Makeham, John. 1994. *Name and Actuality in Early Chinese Thought*. Albany: State University of New York Press.

McKeon, Richard, ed. 1941. *The Basic Works of Aristotle*. New York: Random House.

Moore, Charles, ed. 1986. *The Chinese Mind*. Honolulu: University of Hawaii Press.

Nitobe, Inazo. 1969. *Bushido: The Soul of Japan*. Rutland, Vt.: Charles E. Tuttle Company, Inc.

Oyama, Masutatsu. 1979. *The Kyokushin Way*. Tokyo: Japan Publications.

Pound, Ezra. 1951. *Confucius: The Great Digest & Unwobbling Pivot*. New York: New Directions Books.

Shun, Kwong-loi. 1997. *Mencius and Early Chinese Thought*. Stanford, Calif.: Stanford University Press.

Simpkins, C. Alexander and Annellen M. Simpkins. 1998. *Meditation From Thought to Action*. Boston: Tuttle.

Simpkins, C. Alexander and Annellen M Simpkins. 1999. *Simple Taoism: A Guide to Living in Balance*. Boston: Tuttle.

Siren, Osvald. 1963. *Chinese on the Art of Painting*. New York: Shocken Books.

Smith, Howard D. 1973. *Confucius*. New York: Charles Scribner's Sons.

Smith, Huston. 1991. *The World's Religions*. San Francisco: Harper San Francisco.

Son, Duk Sung, and Robert J. Clark. 1968. *Korean Karate: The Art of Tae Kwon Do*. New York: WTKDA Press, Inc.

Spangler, Todd. "Attitude Linked with Heart Problems." New York: Associated Press.

Spiller, R. E. 1965. *Selected Essays, Lectures, and Poems of Ralph Waldo Emerson*. New York: Pocket Books.

Ssu-ma, Ch'ien and W.H. Nienhauser, ed. 1994. *The Grand Scribe's Records Vol. 1*. Bloomington: Indiana University Press.

Sze, Mai-mai. 1959. *The Way of Chinese Painting*. New York: Vintage Books.

Tat, Wei. 1970. *An Exposition of the I-Ching or Book of Changes*. Republic of China: Institute of Cultural Studies.

Tsunetomo, Yamamoto. 1979. *Hagakure: The Book of the Samurai.* Tokyo: Kodansha International Ltd.

Waley, Arthur. 1946. *Three Ways of Thought in Ancient China.* London: George Allen & Unwin Ltd.

Watson, Burton. 1969. *Hsün Tzu.* New York: Columbia University Press.

Wilhelm, Richard. 1931. *Confucius and Confucianism.* New York: Harcourt Brace Javonovich, Inc.

_____. 1979a. *Lectures on the I Ching: Constancy and Change.* Princeton, N.J.: Princeton University Press

_____, trans. 1979b. *The I Ching or Book of Changes.* Princeton, N.J.: Princeton University Press.

Wilhem, Richard, and Hellmut Wilhelm. 1979. *Understanding the I Ching.* Princeton, N.J.: Princeton University Press.

Wittenborn, Allen. 1991. *Further Reflections on Things at Hand: A Reader Chu Hsi.* Lantham, Md.: University Press of America.

Yearley, Lee H. 1990. *Mencius and Aquinas.* Albany: State University of New York Press.

Yutang, Lin. 1994. *The Wisdom of Confucius.* New York: The Modern Library.

_____. 1942. *The Wisdom of China and India.* New York: Random House.

ALSO BY C. ALEXANDER
AND
ANNELLEN SIMPKINS

Principles of Meditation

•

Zen Around the World

•

Living Meditation

•

Meditation from Thought to Action

•

Simple Taoism

•

Simple Zen

Library of Congress Cataloging-in-Publication Data

Simpkins, C. Alexander.
    Simple Confucianism : a guide to living virtuously / C. Alexander
Simpkins & Annellen Simpkins. — 1st ed.
        p. cm.
    Includes bibliographical references.
    ISBN 0–8048–3177–7 (pbk.)
    1. Confucianism. 2. Conduct of life. I. Simpkins, Annellen M. II. Title.

    BL1852 .S55 2000
    299'.51244—dc21   99–048864